Dedicated to my dear old dad whose battle with cancer gave me the courage to find my voice.

This one's for you pops...

Foreword

The spirit of life is a book of inspiration and meaning. For so long now, man has disconnected further and further from the very essence of his being and in so doing has disconnected from his true purpose – that is to love and be loved and to experience himself in all of his entirety.

To find ones way back to love and back to self, one must first become aware of all that has kept him distracted from his journey. As the wheels of society turn faster and take us further from our truth, one starts to feel a disconnection so big that one can no longer even feel, hear or sense the desperate call of our soul as it asks us to recognise that truth.

To live with love is to live with peace. To understand how to love is to understand how to be at peace. To recognise that we have allowed ourselves to be pulled so far away from love that we can no longer imagine a world that could ever be at peace is to recognise the true failings of our society. The trappings and trimmings that pull us away from a life that is real – a life with purpose and meaning – are the trappings of a society that has come undone. A society that puts wealth over health and the greed of corporations over the need of the individual. A society that takes a creative individual and turns him into part of the conforming masses by crushing the very dreams and passions that he was gifted with at birth. A society that breaks the will of its people by stripping them of all that is real and true and replacing it with convoluted truths that best serve its purpose – that is to control and to separate instead of nurturing and uniting.

The spirit of life is a book that seeks to gently guide man back to this truth by helping him to see how we have come to live in a world whereby we don't even question the 'truths' that we have always been told. It is a book that seeks to inspire man to reconnect with those gifts and passions that have been stripped away and replaced with a need to make money at all costs, whether it be to the detriment of his own soul or that of another.

By gently inspiring man to reconnect with these gifts, this book seeks to re-empower the people to remove the shackles of society and to start to think and feel for themselves again. To allow their senses to guide their way as they begin to reconnect with their soul, instead of listening to what has been cleverly placed in their head. To start to see truth, in all of its entirety, not by teaching them what the truth is, but instead by teaching them how to find it for themselves.

'United we stand, divided we fall' – this book helps to show man the error of his ways. As we disconnect from self, so too do we disconnect from each other. As we give our power away to those that will take it, so too do we allow that power to be used to cause division and hatred in our world. As we refuse to open our eyes to our reality, so too do we refuse to open our eyes to self.

We live in an ever-changing world and each and every individual has the power to change the world for the better. It has been said many times that change must come from within, this book seeks to provoke that change by gently provoking consciousness in a way that has not been seen before. To read this book is the first step to 'being the change that we all wish to see'.

Introduction

'The past is a foreign country, they do things differently there.' I don't think that I ever fully appreciated the magnitude of this statement when I read L.P. Hartley's book The Go-between as part of the school syllabus. Now this statement depicts the enormity of change that has followed me throughout my entire life.

I barely recognise the high flying, materialistic stockbroker that I was only a few years ago, in the hectic storm that is Hong Kong, let alone the young and fragile girl who was bullied at school previously. Change has followed me throughout my whole life and whilst, for a long time, I lived a life shrouded in fear, the one thing that I always intrinsically knew is that change is often for the good. That's not to say that I didn't fight change every step of the way on occasions, particularly when it came to walking away from relationships that were no longer serving me. Instead I would stay and continue to try to salvage whatever I could from the ashes of a destructive relationship, never allowing myself to let go, no matter how much pain it was causing me, not because I was scared of being alone – I already knew that I could do that – but rather because I was fearful of what would be on the other side for me when I had learned to become so comfortable in the situation that I was currently in. Sometimes we convince ourselves that we are happy in our current situations because it just seems easier that way but, often, what lays on the other side of change is the path to finding our dreams, if only we had the courage to take the leap of faith that is needed to get us there.

That doesn't mean that we should berate ourselves for not making these decisions sooner – life is all about timing after all. It is often through the most painful experiences that we learn the most about ourselves. It is in these moments that we find the strength to become who we truly are and it is through these experiences that we, eventually, learn to embrace change for the gift that it is.

It is through such painful experiences that I finally came to find my true self. Six years of ill health took a massive toll on my ability to be the person that I had always believed myself to be. I knew myself to be a wild party girl, sociable to the core and defined by my career as a stockbroker. Designer clothes, sports cars and flash city pads helped me to hide the array of insecurities that I had carried around with me since I was that bullied child. No one could touch me now! The false confidence that I gained from partying even allowed me to hide those insecurities from myself for a time, although, of course, when I look back on my behaviour in those days, it is evident that it was all a direct reaction to the broken person that I had become inside.

No longer able to be the sociable party girl that I once was and finding myself in a new country – a country whose expat community were also fully committed to the party, I found myself facing a massive internal conflict – 'Who am I if not that party girl?' Mentally I was still that person but physically that lifestyle had become impossible for me to lead. This became a great challenge for me as, previously, I had always found myself at the centre of many social circles but now, in this new and unfamiliar country, I also found myself in the unfamiliar territory of being on the outside of a circle of friends due to a lack of energy to socialise.

I became very weak, both physically and mentally. I lost myself in relationships as I no longer had the strength of character to know who I was. I had known for a long time that I was sensitive to the energy of spirit but I had no idea that I was sensitive to the energy of other people too. In my already weakened state, I found that I became heavily bogged down with the energy of others. I found myself drowning in negativity and encased by fear. My overly sensitive body came under a sensory attack, from noise pollution, to light, air and food pollution. Being the perfectionist that I am, I was determined to continue to do my job to a high standard but, whilst keeping up this appearance, I was dying inside. The work that I had previously enjoyed began to drown me in a sea of stress, misery and pain. After four and a half years of working as a stockbroker in Hong Kong, I began to feel that I had sold my soul.

Walking away from that lifestyle and that pay cheque, was one of the hardest decisions, mentally, that I have ever had to make, but, over time, that decision became forced upon me by the state of my health. After six years of living in misery, stress and continuous pain, I walked away from my fifteen year career in finance and I can honestly say that I have never looked back. The poor health that I had always seen as a curse had suddenly become one of the biggest gifts that life had ever given to me.

I embarked on one of the most amazing adventures of my life – an adventure that took me through South and Central America and eventually to a place where I finally started to know who the real me was – warts and all. I have never experienced freedom like it. Not only the freedom to travel without the constraints of work or a time frame but much more importantly, the freedom for my soul to be exactly who it needed to be. I had yearned for this kind of freedom for so long, without ever fully recognising it, and now that it was here, I could not understand why I had let the fear of change control me for so long.

Like most people, my path has been far from easy – from bullying, to ill health, the obligatory heartbreak through lies and deceit and the loss of my father to cancer, there have been times when I have wanted to stand on a rooftop and scream, but the one thing that has always got me through every hardship, including my father's death, is the fact that with every painful experience comes the gift of growth. If we can truly recognise and embrace this gift, instead of wallowing in the self-pity of our lives, then we can walk head on into that gift of change that allows us to follow our dreams. After all, why are we here if not to express every aspect of our soul?

The gift of change has brought me to a place where I finally feel at peace with myself. I feel an inner happiness and understanding that was never available to me before – or at least I didn't think it was. Don't get me wrong, I still have a long way to go on my journey – the journey of self never ends – but instead of feeling like I'm in a constant uphill battle against life, I now feel that everything just falls into place and that everything is as it's meant to be. This is what happens when you walk the path that your soul intended, instead of one shrouded in fear, control and doubt.

That path for me is one of service. I always knew that the first part of my life would be about 'being selfish' and doing what I needed to do to 'fix me' (not that that should ever be considered selfish) and that the second half would be about 'giving back', although I had no idea in what way. Through my South American adventure, I learned that my path would eventually lead me to setting up a school and an orphanage. Whilst I know that this is definitely something that I will do, in all honesty, I just don't feel ready to take on such a big project at this stage in my life. I guess I haven't fully moved out of the 'selfish' stage and into the 'giving' stage just yet!

Instead, my present journey has led me to be of service to spirit, which I hope will eventually be of service to mankind. Spirit has been in my life for as long as I can remember, although I didn't always recognise it as that. In my early twenties, spirit was literally trying to shake me awake but in my comatose state, it took over four years of said shaking until I eventually opened my mind to the possibility of spirit's existence. Living the materialistic lifestyle that I did, I was extremely sceptical of anything even remotely spiritual.

I took a few classes but, to tell you the truth, I just wasn't ready to be a weirdo!! My well-hidden, inward, lack of confidence would not allow me to embrace the 'weirdness within' at that stage of my life and so, I politely asked them to bugger off until I was ready to embrace 'the freakiness'. A request which they graciously honoured. I always knew that the time would come when I would need to reopen that tightly sealed door and I could feel that time looming closer before I left Hong Kong.

I returned to the UK after my travelling adventures and immediately enrolled onto a mediumship class, after much pestering from spirit. I knew, almost immediately, that I would not necessarily be pursuing the role of a medium in the normal sense of the word, that is, bringing people's deceased loved ones through, although it is a skill that I have been honing for the past five years. Instead, I intuitively knew that I would be working with an 'enlightened spirit' and bringing through information to share with the world through writing. I had absolutely no idea how this was going to happen and quite frankly, the idea terrified me – I told you that I was bullied right? The idea of putting myself out there like this to be publicly criticised was not an idea that I relished but, all the same, I knew that it would happen.

After a year and a half of mediumship development, Merlin, the 'enlightened spirit' that I speak of and the very essence of this book, found a way to connect with me through an impromptu trance mediumship session during one of my classes.

Trance mediumship sees the medium and the spirit world blending to a much closer degree than a demonstrating or private sitting medium is able to achieve. Through the deep passive state of trance, where both mental and physical energies are shared, a situation can be created whereby the spirit communicator can directly impact the medium's mind. This allows spirit to communicate directly, eliminating any need for interpretation by the medium.

There are different states of trance, light, medium and deep, so the level of control by spirit can vary. Trance is still a form of mental mediumship so there will always be an element of awareness by the medium as to what is being said, although at a deep level it may only register in the subconscious mind.

Being somewhat of a control freak (and desperately trying to control the process of letting that go) deep trance was not an option for me, and so we gently blended our minds and our souls to a level at which I felt comfortable. It was here that we became at one with each other. I have never felt inner peace and wisdom like it. I had the innate sense that the spirit that had joined me was an incredibly enlightened wizard, which, like you, I also found a little odd!!!

Please don't make the mistake of thinking that I have taken his identity lightly – an identity which I didn't discover until the third time we sat together. Accepting that he is who he says he is has been incredibly difficult for me. Believe me, if I was making this up, I would have gone for a much easier sell than a legendary wizard!

Several months later another trance session presented itself to me and this time the teacher asked us to bring through some words of wisdom from our communicator. I immediately recognised him as being the same enlightened wizard who had joined me previously and as I listened, in my light trance state, to the words of wisdom that my communicator brought forward, I recognised the language being used as being very similar to that which flows through me when I write. I had known for some time that spirit was helping me with my writing but I had no idea that it was this particular spirit who had been helping me all along.

That was when I made the decision to sit with him and write to simply see what would happen. By reading this book, you will bear witness to those conversations from start to finish – no editing, no changing, just as it came!!

During that third session, the first time that we sat together alone, I felt his energy much more strongly than on the previous two sessions and suddenly his energy felt so familiar to me. As I later discovered, through asking personal questions away from this book, we have shared all of our lives together – whether he be my guide, I be his or we reincarnated together. My wisdom is his wisdom and his wisdom is mine. We are a team he and I – always have been and always will be.

The words of wisdom that come from myself and Merlin blending our minds are, for the most part, nothing more than what each and every one of you already knows deep down inside. For some it may be buried much deeper than others and may take a lot more work to reconnect you with that which you already know. Through years of conditioning, we have all been taught to live in fear and negativity and have forgotten how to connect with our soul – the very essence of our being! We have forgotten how to feel and how to think for ourselves and more importantly, we have forgotten how to be the people that we were born to be. This book simply seeks to bring some of that forgotten knowledge into your awareness. If you are able to open your minds, even a little, to the reality of this concept then it shall not take long for you to be able to see that, that which is being shown to you is nothing but truth. I am a conduit for the words for the path to change – the rest is up to you…

I realise that this book may come under some harsh criticism. There will be those who call this book blasphemous, or even just a crock of shit and there is nothing that I can do to change that, but I ask you, even if you can't believe that these words came from spirit, is the very essence of the message being delivered really so difficult to believe? Is it so hard to believe that living from your heart rather than your head could bring about the changes that our world so desperately needs to see? Do you really believe that the current system that we live under is fair for all? Do you truly believe that change is impossible, or is that just what we are led to believe? If you are unable to open your mind to spirit, please allow this book to open your mind to change. It is time to embrace the change that is undoubtedly coming. Instead of fighting against that change, allow yourselves to be part of it – the change into consciousness. The change for humanity. The change that will allow you to follow your dreams and create a better future for all.

And so our journey begins...

25th May 2015

Giving and loving and living and sharing – this is all that anyone can ask. Living in love instead of living in fear – making decisions from that place of love rather than fear is all that is needed to change our fates. To change humanity and to create peace all one must do is bring themselves back to a place of love. To re-centre the Earth we first must re-centre ourselves.

To give with love, to BE with love and to live with love is to create the kind of change that will bring humanity to salvation.

We are powerful creative beings – our powers are within our thoughts. Our thoughts have been hijacked over many years to think negatively and without reason. To think negatively is to create disempowerment and a world full of fear. And so you see, the circle goes on, round and round it goes until one day it is gently broken by love.

When love truly arrives in our hearts and in our minds, only then shall we reap all the love that we have sown, for to be without love is to be without life. Love is the life force of all things whilst fear creates death and darkness. Move into the light by moving into love, for after all, the only thing that is real is love…

Dance my dear, dance under the stars, bare all to the brightness of the sky. Do not be afraid to be all that you are and to share that with the world. When you are strong and confident in yourself, so shall it be done in others. You are a star so bright but that brightness is dimmed by fear.

Let go my dear, surrender and embrace all that you are and all that you can be, for all that you can be is greatness.

Dance in the rain, be naked and feel the rain drops touch your skin, for when you allow yourself to feel touched by the rain, so too will you feel the touch of others. Do not be afraid to be the sexual being that you are – release the shackles of bondage that past lives have encompassed you in.

To create fully you must know and experience the magnitude of the sexual being that you are. Make love to the rain and it shall make love back. Let the sun caress you and the wind dishevel you and never be afraid to cry out with pleasure, for it is these pleasurable moments that release the true depths of your being. When you can release this passion inside of yourself, so too will you be able to surrender to spirit and reach your full potential, that is, to love and to heal and to be loved and be healed. So trust in me, sit with me, do not be afraid of the things that I ask you to do for all that I ask you to do is all that you need to do to become truly enlightened and truly at one with yourself and the universe.

Dismiss not your gifts for you truly are a gifted being – strong in charm and strong in love and these are the gifts that will bring your true powers to the surface and allow them to shine in a world that shies away with fear. Be who you are and love with all your heart, for you are loved and you are supported and protected and under our protection, no harm can come to you.

Embrace all that comes your way, the good and the bad, for they are all lessons in love. Resistance can only bring pain whilst acceptance brings power. Power must be used in the right way but in you we trust. Let go of the ego that keeps you from surrendering – you are an ambassador of spirit and in you we have high hopes.

Thank you my dear, thank you for your time and your dedication and thank you for sitting with me. I am glad that we are now united for we have much work to do together. Come back tomorrow my dear and we shall continue with our journey. I hope that puts your mind at rest, for I understand that you have some fear but trust in me and our journey together can begin… Much love my dear…

Your dear friend, Merlin, the magic man.

26th May 2015

Rest my dear, for we still have much work to do. Do not be hard on yourself for not surrendering straight away – do you think that Buddha was able to give himself so freely without practise? Greatness takes time and patience my dear and you shall get there when the time is right.

For now, please come back and sit with me every day so that we can work together on your resistance. Cherish each moment, for learning is part of the journey and as you know, it is the journey not the destination that's important.

Your time to shine will come my dear. For now, let us sit quietly together each day and just allow what happens to happen. Try not to resist. Allow me to be gentle with you, for the subtlety of energy is what you need to understand to be able to work with it. I don't want to be rough with you my dear, I simply want you to feel my gentle caress and respond to it as a lover would respond to the touch of her beloved.

Gentle be it that you may become familiar with me, to know me, to sense me, to feel me even when you don't know that I am there, for I am always there and will always be with you, holding your hand as a true friend should.

Never fear for I will always be with you, gently guiding you through life's journeys. You will never be alone.

Let us sit and contemplate for a minute the learning that today's session has brought. You have learnt that resistance is futile and does not take you closer to your desired goal. Be in the moment and ask for nothing – allow what is meant to happen to happen, for only then will you see all that is waiting to be shown to you.

The astral travelling will come my dear – do keep practising but don't expect results too quickly. True greatness comes from lots of practise. Just appreciate the subtle energies that come over you and learn to recognise each feeling, each touch. You have needed to be grounded for some time now to deal with all that has come your way but now you are free to move forward with your journey – a journey of greatness and wonderment, for your goal is to reach enlightenment. As you know, you have been there before but must now bring the other soul that you helped there as well.

You are so close – it is in your reach if only you could fight the urge to resist. Together we shall overcome this, day by day, patiently training until you are able to breathe in the light again and let go of all the darkness that you still hold onto. Be free my dear, be free. Release all anguish and fear and return back to the state of pure love that you were once before.

The journey of your soul has been turbulent my dear but never anything that you were not able to handle. You are strong and you are wise and you have so much knowledge and wisdom to share with the world, as much you know, but you must first unlock the passion within you that has already stirred. Stand in your own power and be a force to be reckoned with. But gently does it as with great power comes great responsibility and you must be ready to deal with it wisely.

And so, as our session today comes to a close, let me leave you with this thought – you are the light, you are the love, you are the darkness and you are the fear but love shall always overcome if only you would give yourself willingly to me, my beautiful Guinevere.

27th May 2015

Love my dear is a tenuous word – it can be full of pain and heartache and full of joy and pleasure all at the same time. But you see my dear, this is what makes us who we are. It is what we live for. To FEEL that pain and experience that pleasure, for without these things, who are we really? We are the love and we are the light. We are the shadow and we are the darkness. We are all these things encompassed and so shall we be all that we can be when we allow ourselves to be touched by the hands of God, in all of its glory and all of its pain, for to be love and to be fear is to be God.

To know who we truly are we first must experience all things. To be God, we must be all things. Step out of the fear for it is now time to shine – in love and in joy and in all things pure, for it is time for the light to rise again from your soul – step into the light, it is calling you back, for you have been away for too long. Don't worry my dear, all things in their right time but now is your time my dear, now is your time.

Love with an open heart and forgive in the same way. Let go of past pain that still causes you anguish and torment, for you already know that your teacher is your soul mate. Worry not, for he will be ok – he too will find the light and your love will be reunited once more when the time is right. Do not shy from your destiny my dear – embrace it with open arms.

Words are your master but they are your downfall too. Many times have your words seen your tongue cut from your mouth and had you experience torture worse than any man could imagine. Your words are your gift and they are your weapon too – you must learn to use them wisely and freely too. Some time will this take as you free yourself from past torment and fear. Trust in me always and you will have no reason to fear.

Write my dear, write with all of your heart – I am here to help you master your art. You write with such grace and ease and flow but one day you must too speak with such confidence and grace, as you already know. Slowly my dear will you reach your goal but for now dear do not allow it to take its toll. When the time is right you will be ready to go and then my dear the words will simply flow.

For today I feel that I have answered your questions – let us re-adjourn tomorrow in love and in trust and let us strengthen this bond as in me you can trust. And remember my dear, that to surrender is not to lose oneself but instead to find oneself. Together our power is great and so we will work hand in hand, in love and in respect for the greater good. Do not be afraid…

27th May 2015 (afternoon)

Thank you for returning for a second time today my dear – your dedication is noted. With each commitment that you make to sit with me, we move closer to our goal. Soon you will be free of the bondage of fear that keeps you from fulfilling your true potential.

Slowly, slowly we will reach our goal and you will blossom into that which you are here to be. Worry not, for time is on our side and greatness will be achieved.

Let us leave it there for today my dear and we will resume tomorrow our practice. Be happy with what you have achieved today and know that we are on our way to great things. Hold love in your heart my dear, for my love is always yours.

28th May 2015

Frustration my dear – yes let it all out, for here you hold centuries and centuries of shame, humiliation and doubt. And as these seeds of imperfection start to fall from the womb, so too shall you be free of the shame that was thrust upon you by those who knew not what they did, for thine is the Kingdom, the power and the glory through wisdom and freedom and love.

Let it go my dear, let it go. Let the floodgates open and let the darkness be expelled from your soul. You no longer need to carry the guilt of past lives gone. Let it go my dear, let it go. All will be well…

Our work today was gentle but powerful. I stepped aside and only touched you gently to allow you to work. I know the gentleness of this connection has left you struggling to hear my words but look at what you have already achieved today – the beginning of a release so passionate that all inside of you will shake. Let it go my dear, let it go. Be gentle with yourself but do let it go…

29th May 2015

Quiet contemplation leads to release as we unlock the secrets buried beneath. Let go of the anguish buried inside, then my dear you will come alive. Alive for the moment, alive for the now, always being present and filled with love.

Give your love freely, give all that you have to give, for you will always be replenished with God's earthly gifts. Fill your heart with magic and love, for the world is a magical place if only you would let go.

Fear not for the frustration and resistance you feel, soon will it be gone and our journey together can begin. Great things will be achieved with an open heart and mind but first you must leave all your woe behind.

Love like you have never been hurt and extend that love to all around you. Love will not only set you free but your love will set others free too. Chained are the masses to bondage and fear but once you break free of it my dear your journey will be clear. Do unto others as you would have them do unto you and forgive all those around you, not just a few.

Bring love and peace into the hearts of others, for love is the only way to turn things around. If you want to save this planet of yours, restore man to peace and harmony and natural laws. Bring balance back into hearts and minds and remind people often that they need to be kind. Kind to themselves and to each other too – all of these things are within you to do.

Love my dear, love and be loved – cherish your moments and find joy in the small things. Bathe in the sweet perfume of the flowers, take in the midnight sky and allow the sun to touch your skin.

Fear not others' opinions, for when you are grounded and connected and truly at ease, you will know that the opinion of others only comes from a place of fear. To open the hearts of others, your heart must first be opened too – you're getting there my dear but still much work we must do…

Let us leave our session there for today – walk away open and ready to embrace the day. Challenges may come but remember to always be kind, for it is in these small acts yourself you shall find.

1st June 2015

Gentle does it and gentle be it and soon shall you look back and see how far you have come, for even small steps will see you reach the top of the summit. Spend your time wisely and give your time generously, for the moments that you spend with me are most precious indeed.

Freedom will come as you conquer your fears, and stepping into your power will become so simple my dear. Laugh like you mean it and stand strong in your beliefs, for rhyme can be without reason when one's soul is shrouded in fear. Let not what others think, feel or say allow you to hold yourself back from going on your way. You hold the key to the truth in your heart but to get to it you must first release yourself from the trappings of the past.

Trust in yourself and in the process too, for to be honest dear, there is nothing else you can do. Others' truths are their truths in fear, they too must unlock the shackles of society's teachings for all to become clear. You have the wisdom, the strength and the courage to aid them on their way but first you too must be clear about what it is that you need to say. To find the truth you must first find yourself fully – you're nearly there my dear, there's no need to worry.

Release the fear of past lives gone, now is the time to bring centuries of learning into fruition. Shine you will through the darkness that may proceed, for things may get worse and the Earth may bleed, but from the ashes will the proverbial phoenix rise and no longer will your race stand for the lies.

Strength is in numbers as you already know, so continue to help man rise from their slumber and stand hand in hand against corporate propaganda. United as one you can be the thunder, the wind and the rain – mighty in numbers and mighty in strength, united like this, no longer in fear and repent.

Together in numbers you all can shine, so come together as one spirit, one mind. Alone you are not in this mission you hold, for there are many others to lighten the load. Step into your power as they step into theirs and watch the magic happen as the knowledge starts to take seed.

Awaken, awaken, you all must awaken, as the Earth starts to move into a higher vibration, so too must its inhabitants to create harmony and peace, for as we leave this time of war and destruction so too shall we leave behind greed and fear and instead work together collectively for the greater good of all mankind.

Selfishness is created by separation from source so let us reunite ourselves with not only the power of our master but also the power of each other. Together we must come in love and in trust, for to move things forwards these things are a must. This may seem impossible but you will see one day, that all that I say is achievable through the higher vibration of love.

2nd June 2015

I appreciate you finding time to sit with me today – I know it wasn't easy to do but still you came. So much closer do we move to our desired goal. Many things will we, together, achieve as you move towards your destiny. It's at your fingertips now my dear – all you have to do is reach.

We come into this world with such love and such beauty. As our mother lifts us from the midwife's arms and cradles us close to her breast, we have no fear for all that we know is love my dear. But as we grow, we begin to feel the woe, of the disconnections and fear that have already been sewn into those that we trust with our care. Soon too will we be filled with the fears and opinions of the people that we love, who may love us dearly too but who unwittingly do us a magnitude of disservice by encroaching their fears upon us. For rather than allowing us to stay connected to our heart and soul, instead we are ripped from that which keeps us protected and whole and would lead us into a life without fear.

In this way, we find ourselves united with an ego that holds such might that it believes itself to always be right. No room is there for intuition and love, instead only fear, self-doubt and hatred. Hatred towards those who think differently to us or to those who may threaten our ego with gifts different to ours, for whilst our ego protects as well, it only knows how to protect itself.

As the ego connects itself to body and mind, to the soul it becomes nothing but blind. As the disconnect between soul and mind strengthens, so too does the bond between man and God weaken. To find our way back to God, we must first find our way back to our own soul. Our soul holds all the answers to the questions asked, all of the answers, future, present and past. For to reconnect with the beauty of one's own soul, is the whole purpose of life on this plane, it's our only goal.

Love, laugh, cry and scream, sing at the top of your voice and remember to dream. Feel with everything that you do and listen carefully as your soul rings true. Reconnect with the things that you love and let your soul shine brightly with this gift from above.

Never stop mastering your art, for your gifts are the key to unlocking your heart. As your heart unlocks so too will the love explode and those around you will be touched and inspired to unlock that that has kept them surrounded by chains – chains of misfortune, misery and pain. And as once again we begin to connect, finding our passions and moving out of our head, the truth will become clear for all to see, that is my dear, that we must simply BE. Be who we are instead of being who we are not, as you see my dear, this happens a lot. As the ego takes hold, as surely it does, we become who we are told to be instead of who we were born to be. Step out of this darkness and back into the light, let us learn again how to live our lives right. Don't be afraid, for change is good but change must be all encompassing and brought about from a place of love.

3rd June 2015

'Who am I' you ask, as we release the memories of lives past, memories entrenched deep in your cells, triggering reactions like Pavlov's bells. You are the earth, the sky, the wind and the rain, you are the all and the nothing as you endure torture and pain. You are the stars in the sky and you are the earth on the ground, you are all of these wonders going round and round. You are everything and you are nothing, you are love and you are fear, you are the winter and the summer, for you are God my dear.

God is the earth, the wind and the rain. God is the love, the fear and the pain. God is the gentle touch on your skin, God is the all, God is everything.

We are all tiny fragments of God, bursting with unlimited potential. We limit ourselves to the stars in the sky, limiting ourselves with the hows and the why. We are everything, we are everywhere, a soul of truth ready to be laid bare. Through each of our lives, we learn precious lessons which add to our soul's eternal presence.

Connect to yourself, deeply you must delve, to release yourself from the shackles. The how and the why, it's all by and by – deeply you must go to just let it all go. Deeper, deeper to the depths of your soul, releasing the blackness and darkness that has taken its toll. All of the pain have you had to endure, to bring you back to a place that is pure. Without the darkness there can be no light but let it go now my dear, let it go with all your might.

Soon you will stand in your power so strong, it will soon be time my dear, it will not be long. Until then continue to work on dispelling the pain, soon you will be rid of past life shame. Step into the light, you have nothing to fear, for hand in hand we will walk my dear.

4th June 2015

Is magic real is the question you ask, well my dear, you present me with quite a task, for first we must understand what magic is. Magic is around us every day, magic touches us in the sunshine's ray. Magic is in the air that we breathe, magic is a raindrop on the autumn leaf. Magic is in a lover's touch, magic is in the nature that you love so much. Magic is birth, life and death, magic is the feeling of love in our chest. Possess ye much magic in the touch of your hand, surrounded by magic as your feet touch the land. Magic is in every thing that we do, lest ye have forgotten, your common man too…

Magic is the creation of thought, magic is forgotten in all that you are taught. It may be so that common man has forgotten how to use magic, but those who are most powerful on your planet have not. They know very well how to use the magic of creative thought to keep you on the lower vibration of fear, but as I keep saying, all you need is love my dear. Return to the higher vibration of love and return to the magic, your birth-right from above.

Watch the magic return to the land, feel it in every grain of sand. Spread the magic wand of love, look up and see the spread wings of a dove. Watch the magic return to the Earth, no longer treat it as a monetary worth. See the magic touch mankind, leave all your fear and worries behind.

Allow the magic to wash over you, feel it in every thing that you do. Then will you see that your planet regrows, leaving behind all of its current woes. Flourish again will the strength of the trees, working together with the birds and the bees. No longer will the Earth shake with such might, for you see my dear, it's been given quite a fright. Bled of its resources through power and greed, never any time to take stock and reseed. Shaking with trepidation is your beautiful land, as it asks you to simply walk hand in hand.

Love, as always, will conquer all, love is all you need, it's the magical ball. So feel that magic coursing through your veins, learn to master the magic and release the chains. Allow me to touch you with this magic so true, then I promise my dear, you will know what to do…

5th June 2015

We work together hand in hand as our minds blend into one. My thoughts are your thoughts and your thoughts are my thoughts as we merge our minds to find the rhymes. My truth is your truth and your truth is my truth and that truth my dear is love. Love is the one and only truth and soon the world will have its proof, as the world unites hand in hand and realigns with the land.

Matter not how one finds the love, just follow the guidance from above. As the barriers of separation start to fall between race, colour and creed, allow the seed of love to grow into perfect harmony. Matter not religion, country or sex, the act of love demands no checks. Embrace each other with open arms, allow yourselves to see each other's charms. You are all God's children, black, white and poor, upon each other do not shut the door.

Stand together in unity, be true to God and you will see. To be true to God is to be true to yourself, this will lead you back to mental health. Restore yourself back to natural balance, this may be the biggest challenge, but as you reconnect with source, no longer will you feel remorse. Reconnect yourself with love, reconnect with your Lord above.

No expectations of you will there be, expectations are created by man you see. Kept in fear and kept in chains, usually for other peoples' gains. Set yourself free from these teachings, no Godly law will you be breeching. Simply reconnect with love, that is the only hope from above.

Come together, stand as one, unity consciousness can be done. Stand together in love so strong and all your fears and worries will be gone. Reconnect with the Earth's natural joys, leave behind your material toys. The Earth will provide you with all that you need, but we need to get back to its natural seed. Man's greed destroys the Earth day by day, soon to be left in a state of decay. Come together hand in hand, there is still time to save this beautiful land.

5th June 2015 (afternoon)

How will love turn evil hearts? Surely it's written in the charts? How will love save the day? Surely wrongdoers they must pay? How will love change the world? Surely too many toes have curled? How will love mend our pain? Surely it's entrenched in our brain? How will love see us back to glory? Surely it's too late to change this story? How will love make us whole? For surely that's the only goal?

Love will help a voice be heard, love will separate you from the herd. Love will hear another soul's pain, love will help them to unlock the chain. Love will hear another soul's cry, love will look them in the eye. Love will feel the stretch of open arms, love will help them recognise their charms. Love will keep them from straying away, love will hear what they have to say. Love will walk with them through the darkness, love will bring them back to a place of calmness. Love will hear the soul's initial cry, love will reach them before they're entangled in the lie.

Turn ye not your back in hate, for then love will reach them way too late. Do not deafen your ears from a struggling soul's cry, for then you give them an alibi. As we hear of another bleed, do not forget we may have sown that seed. If we do not draw a line in the sand, then we may find that we have blood on our hand. Do not turn your back in hate, do not seal another's fate.

Come together in love so grand, see it spread throughout the land. Come together in love so great, see how love can change your fate. Come together in love so strong, see how love knows right from wrong. Come together in love so proud, see how love unites the crowd. Come together in love so true, this is all that you need to do…

6th June 2015

I am who I say I am my dear, I know you have doubt and a little fear. How will you explain it away? What will all of those people say? Merlin the magic man I am, the legend is real, it's not a sham. King Arthur's knights and a table so round, if you look for evidence it can be found.

As man lost his love for magic, the story became a little tragic, for much information was buried and the use of magic became heavily levied. Branded witches and burnt at the stake, so much power did they take. The knowledge of magic ripped from our hands, the knowledge of magic banished from all the lands.

Magic lost from our memories, magic seeing us fall to our knees. Magic labelled a tool of the devil, magic switched to a whole new level. Magic became a thing of legends, never again to be openly mentioned. Magic lost from our minds forever, magic oh what a beautiful treasure.

Magic was the master of the land, magic happened at the flick of a hand. Magic was something to truly be mastered, losing magic was such a disaster. As many a man moved from his heart, lost was the beauty of this treasured art. As man used magic for personal gain, man brought about torture and pain. As man used magic to further his cause, man broke many spiritual laws. As man used magic against his fellow man, harder it was to be who I am. No longer could magic be used in such ways, tragic it was to leave those days. Magic when used for the good of mankind, no better a tool will you find.

Embrace the legend that I am, the legend of Merlin the magic man. Know that I speak the truth, search and ye shall find the proof. Matter not who I am, but do know that magic's not a sham.

Magic is yours to use, if this is the path that you so choose. Close your eyes and ask for help, take your magic book down from the shelf. Use the magic of creative thought, this is a skill that cannot be bought. Available it is to all mankind, simply look and ye shall find. Reconnect yourself back with this power, rebuild your ivory tower. Embrace the truth in all of its glory, then you will know the entire story.

7th June 2015

Always, always speak from your heart, this is how you will play your part. Your part in saving this beautiful Earth, as it goes through a complete rebirth. At higher levels must it vibrate, man too before it's too late. Hold your arms out in love, put your trust in God above.

How many natural disasters must there be, for man to realise there's no harmony? How many more times must the Earth shake, for man to realise that it's about to break? How many more fish must be washed ashore, before man realises he's polluting the core? How many more animals must die, before we give something else a try?

Return mankind back to natural laws, help him to recognise society's flaws. Bring Earth back to its natural seed, help man recognise Monsanto's greed. Guide man away from factory farming, this is an industry that's truly alarming. Open the eyes of those around you, take man back to what he once knew.

Science with all of its marvels, often disguising all of its foibles. Man puts such trust in science, even when man works in defiance. Messing around with human genetics, filing your bodies with toxic synthetics. Ignoring all of the flaws in your plan, doing things just because you believe that you can. Science is an incredible wonder, but messing with nature will bring about thunder. Much like magic when in the wrong hands, science will destroy your beautiful lands.

Return to nature, back to natural laws, in nature you will find there are no flaws. Return to nature, live off the land, work with nature hand in hand. Return to nature, gently with love, live off of the gifts provided from above. Return to nature, improve your health, no longer create others' wealth. Return to nature and all of its healing, and soon you'll get back to your natural feeling. Numb with chemicals for the pain, these are just another chain. Free yourselves from synthetic flaws, re-embrace natural laws.

8th June 2015

The age old question of karma, always causes such a drama. Twisted does man have the issue, but that is why I am here to assist you. For every action that you take, an equal and opposite effect you make. For everything that you do, that will affect another too. For every decision that you make, another course does your life take. For every new door that you open, your original path will be broken. For every wrongdoing that you do, that will come right back to you. For every dream that's set in motion, that's just a drop in the great big ocean.

It is the soul's choice, have no doubt, as to whether or not it works its karma out. The soul will always see the beauty, in living out its karmic duty. The soul makes decisions based on trust, and understands that karma is a must. To experience itself in all of its glory, karma is part of the bigger story. To know itself deeply, fully and truly, sometimes it behaves a little unruly.

To know who you are, you must first know who you are not, you must understand that each life is just a tiny little dot. A dot in a universe vast and wide, each life must you ride along with the tide. As the soul uses each life to work out its flaws, it's simply complying with spiritual laws.

Life after life after life will it take, to never make another mistake. Mistakes are part of the learning curve, a part of the process that you don't want to swerve. With each and every mistake that you make, another course of action becomes available to take. With every different path that you choose, there's always the chance that yourself you could lose. With every new role of the dice, the same mistakes may be repeated thrice. With every decision taken anew, you understand more what you need to do. With every action that sees you fall to your knees, you know a little more about who you want to be. With every action that makes your heart feel warm, back to source you feel drawn. With every action that makes you feel shame, on yourself you lay the blame.

Deep into the journey must you go, many seeds must you sow. It's all part of knowing who you are, you set yourselves a very high bar. Easier are the soul's decisions, in working out its future missions, when it's not in human form, and it steps away from life's hectic storm.

Deep, deep, deep must you go, continuously giving the dice another throw. More, more, more will you learn, at each and every difficult turn. Darker, darker, darker will it get, with all of life's lessons that you choose to forget. Lighter, lighter, lighter will it be, as you open your eyes and begin to see.

Karma is a beautiful thing, karma helps your soul remember to sing. Karma is part of the story, karma brings your soul back to its former glory. Karma is a spiritual shower, karma helps you stand in your power. Karma is good for the soul, karma helps you reach your goal. Karma is love so true, karma helps you do what you need to do.

Judge not someone working out their karma, for still may they be an absolute charmer. Shine may their soul incredibly bright, even when in this life they have turned from the light. Choosing to live a life shrouded in darkness, may bring their soul incredible calmness. Restoring balance back to their soul, this is always the ultimate goal. To know who they are, fully, deeply and truly, even when being a little unruly.

To find the light on the darkest day, past convictions they will slay. To find the light through the tragedy, that is life's 'Bohemian Rhapsody'. To find the light from a place of pain, that is the soul's biggest gain. To find the light, to find the trust, that is life's biggest must. To reconnect yourself back with God, to some may seem a little odd, but to be yourself, to live with truth, this will bring you all the proof, for once yourself you understand, with God you will walk hand in hand.

8th June 2015 (afternoon)

Still you fill yourself with worry, that no one will believe you in a hurry. Still in yourself you do not trust, with this knowledge that has been thrust. Still in yourself you do not believe, in all of the things that we shall achieve. Still you fill yourself with fear, that the crowd will surely leer. Still you worry about your fate, that you will invoke people's hate.

Worry not my dear for you hold the ace, you know that there is more than just this physical place. Themselves do they hurt as they turn away in fear, ignoring that which they do not wish to hear. The calm of the night and the calm of the storm, between the two they are deeply torn. Pushing all logic away, scared of changing the state of play. Not knowing that what they don't understand, is aiding in destroying this beautiful land. Burying their heads deep in the sand, instead of standing together hand in hand. Worry not for you shall help them find their way, soon enough will be the day, when all of you stand in your power so strong, when all of you know right from wrong.

No longer will the leaves fall from the trees, no longer will humanity be on its knees. Salvation comes in mysterious ways. Salvation is coming one of these days. Help you will to bring about this magic, so that the state of the Earth is no longer so tragic. Help you will to make man see, no longer is this the way to be. Help you will to open man's eyes, to help him to see all of the lies. Help you will to open man's heart, and reunite him with his art. For each and every one of you has a gift, a gift that will help to mend the rift. A gift that will help you to reunite, and create a future oh so bright.

All of this is in your reach, with your knowledge you must teach. Embrace all of your ancient wisdom, teach them how to implement a different system. The seed of change is on its way, to bring about a brand new day.

10th June 2015

Much clearing was done today my dear. Very deep did we go, to the depths of your soul. Very intense was this session to connect with your lessons in love and in life and in truth.

Love opens your heart, attraction is the dart that allows you to feel excitement and pain. Through new bonds forming, a new day is dawning and much can be achieved.

Step into your power, no longer cower, open up your heart and let love in. To connect with another, to take a lover, none of this is a sin. Embrace your fate, don't close the gate on fun and on laughter and love.

Love can be grand like an orchestral band or can be small like a young child's call. Either way, no matter, as love can surely shatter the fear that you have built up inside.

Allow the touch of a hand, four feet in the sand, two souls uniting as one. Allow the feel of your skin to let love in as it tingles at the sound of a voice. Allow your laughter to bellow like the sound of a cello as you feel yourself make this choice. The choice to let love touch your heart, to feel it like an engine start as your body smiles with delight.

As two souls unite, the light shines so bright on everything that you do. The power of two, with so much to do brings about magic and light. The power of two, with so much to do will bring the gift of sight. The power of two, with so much to do can help a world unite.

So open your heart, grab that dart, do not be afraid of the change. Sit tight, the time is right for you to open yourself up to your fate.

Embrace all that comes your way, stand up and be ready to have your say. The world will soon see you with different eyes, the world will soon see through the lies. A beacon of hope will you be, a kind of spiritual celebrity.

Your love will help to change the world, the magic wand will be twirled. Your love will help man stand as one and move away from society's con. Your love will help day by day but soon you must have your say, for what good is a voice so true and proud until you use it strong and loud? What good is a voice so full of wisdom if you continue to be so fearsome?

Connect with love, connect with another soul, this will help you to reach your goal. For you to connect with another in love will help you stand strong in your power from above. You have much power on your own but to surrender to love you must be shown. No need to worry where it's going, just go in the direction that the wind is blowing. Deep and far or short and near, still will it touch you and release your fear. Intense and strong or fun and light, still will it show you how to take flight. So trust in me and trust in love, embrace this gift from God above. Trust in me, then you will see that love will set you free.

11th June 2015

Today you felt the touch of my hand, as I taught you to use my magic wand. Today you felt the power of my love, as I lay upon you my golden glove. Today you felt the power that is yours, but only to be used for a good cause. Today you put your trust in me, today you will start to be set free.

Today you had a little doubt, today you questioned inside and out. Today you listened as I spoke, today you thought my words were a joke. Today you asked me to touch your face, to reiterate my words just in case. Today my dear you shall see, that my words will set you free. Today my dear you will know, that I would never stoop so low, as to tell you lies, whilst singing you gentle lullabies.

Today my dear you will hear, and you will release a little more fear. Today my dear you will no longer question, anything I tell you in our session. Today my dear you will no longer shy, as you realise my words are not a lie. Today my dear you will no longer fight, as you will see that my words are always right.

Magic is a wondrous gift, magic gives you quite the lift. Magic is a wondrous thing, much joy can it bring. Magic is a powerful tool, a tool that we bestow on you. Magic is an art to be mastered, never to be attempted when you are plastered. Magic must only be practiced with love, a gift bestowed on you from your Lord above.

Here I am to help you master this gift, to help you use it to mend the rift. To bring together all mankind, to leave the dark days far behind. Here I am to help you use this tool, to move the Earth from unfair rule. Here I am to help you to understand the art, of using magic from the heart. Here I am to set you free, and teach you how to simply be. Here I am to help you stand in your power, to open you up like a beautiful flower. Here I am to help you shine so brightly, this is not a task that I shall take lightly.

Hand in hand we shall stay, to bring the Earth a brighter day. Hand in hand we will work, our responsibility we will not shirk. Hand in hand we will be, until we set the world free. Hand in hand we will go, until we move from a vibration oh so low. Hand in hand we will stand, until salvation is restored to the land.

So trust in me, trust in us, allow yourself to feel the buzz. Trust in me, trust in our goal, it is the yearning of your soul. Trust in me, trust in your gift, and see how we shall mend the rift. Trust in me and trust in love, trust in the magic from above. Trust in me and trust in glory, see how love will change this story.

12th June 2015

Another session oh so deep, today have you made a giant leap. Letting go of past mistakes, letting go of tormenting aches. Blocked energy in your back, from all those lives spent on the rack.

Somewhere must that energy go, as it moves about to and fro. Somewhere must that energy be, as we release it from your knee. Somewhere must that energy rest, as we pull it from your chest. Somewhere must that energy move, as your soul we start to soothe. Soon enough it will be dispelled, released from the places that it's held. Soon enough will it be let go, allowing your energy to freely flow.

Yesterday you had your proof, yesterday you had your truth. Yesterday you heard my words, as clearly as the chirping birds. Yesterday you smiled so brightly, as my words touched you lightly. Yesterday you had your answer, now you know I'm not a chancer.

So let's move forward, strong and true, put your trust in all I do. So let's move forward hand in hand, let's move forward without demand. Please remove doubt from your mind, to you I will be nothing but kind. Please leave your fear at the door, spread your wings and you will soar. Please leave your nerves behind, for this we need a clear mind. Please leave your untrusting nature, and know that together we will be greater.

Today your mind is a little clattered, my words are reaching you a little scattered. Today you struggle to hear the rhymes, today your ego slowly climbs. For today, simply you must rest, no need to put me to the test. Tomorrow we will start anew, tomorrow we will see a whole new you.

Allow time for the energy to be released, time to let go of the energetic beast. Rest tonight for I can see that you're tired, the release has left you feeling a little wired. Come back tomorrow rested and calm, tonight you will sleep like a babe in the arm. Come back tomorrow feeling at peace, soon will your troubles cease.

13th June 2015

Still further we must go, to reach the very depths of your soul. Still deeper must we be, to truly set you free. Still more fear must be released, to let go of your past life beliefs. Still more energy must be shifted, before you can feel yourself being uplifted. Still more pain must be dispelled, so that you are no longer a captive held.

You're starting to feel this energetic shift, soon you will see it as a gift. You're starting to know that it's not just for show, as all is released that keeps you low. You're starting to see that you will soon be, a bird that flies oh so free. You're starting to hear the release of your fear, that will move you towards much more cheer. You're starting to open your heart in love, soon you will be as free as a dove.

Step by step we walk our path, no longer feeling your own wrath. Day by day we make our way, until you find you can have your say. Hour by hour we merge our minds, new ways of working together will we find. Minute by minute we blend our souls, to help us achieve our intended goals.

Soon you will be on your way, soon the world will see a brighter day. Soon you will be free from fear, soon you will be a true seer. Soon you will be free from pain, soon you will work towards mankind's gain. Soon you will stand in your power so strong, the time is soon dear, it won't be long.

Let's leave it there for today, there's not much more that I can say, for once you stand in your power so true, you will understand more of what you need to do. Once your fear you have released, you will move back to a place of peace. As peace is love and love is peace, all your doubts will surely cease. As peace is love and love is peace, you're true potential will be released. As peace is love and love is peace, you will achieve your goals with gentle ease.

Trust that we are very close, as your faith in me grows. Trust that we are very near, as you release the final shackles of fear. Trust that we are almost there, to the place that you will dare, to stand in your power oh so strong, and lead the world away from all that is wrong. Trust that we will almost be, working together in harmony. Trust in me and trust in love, trust in your gifts from the Lord above.

14th June 2015

The flow of the wand in your hand, is the first thing that you must command. Gently, gently flicking the wrist, gentle like love's first kiss. Slowly, slowly you will be trained, many lessons will be gained. Open your mind to this gift, I know that you feel a little miffed. This gift is yours if you so choose, give it a go, you have nothing to lose.

I know you still think that it's a little crazy, your memory of magic is a little hazy, but this is a gift that you have always had, but in lives past it was labelled as bad. Many a time burnt at the stake, too many chances did you take. Now you are alive in a different time, now magic is no longer a crime.

Open yourself up in truth, soon magic will give you the proof. I know it seems a little strange, maybe even a little deranged, but as you open yourself up to me, so much more is there for you to see. As you open yourself up to me, the more yourself you can truly be.

Magic isn't just casting spells, and conjuring up potions with all kinds of smells. Magic is a golden gift, magic will help you to mend the rift. Magic can recreate love, in the right direction you it will shove. Magic is the flick of a hand, to bring back harmony to the land. Magic is a powerful word, that allows your wisdom to be heard. Magic is more than just a trick, the art of magic is all in the flick.

Close ye not your mind in wonder, this would be a massive blunder. So much power do you have, to be used without wrath. So much love must you use, magic is not a tool to abuse. So much trust must you show, before you will be ready to give it a go. So much negativity must you dispel, before your friends you'll be ready to tell.

So much more is there to do, before I can fully open up to you. So much more must you learn, many lessons at every turn. So much more open must you be, before you can be totally free. When you are, you will see, all the wonders that you can be. When you are, you will know, and others you will be able to show. When you are, you will embrace, then the world you will be ready to face.

Until then just trust in me, trust in all the things that you see. Let us practise day by day, as gentle as the sun's ray. Let us practise when we sit, learning more bit by bit. Let us practise when you close your eyes, soon you will know that it's not lies. Let us practise when you're still, soon magic your heart will fill.

An open mind is a must, you know by now that in me you can trust. Step away from what you've been taught, you mustn't let your mind be caught. Step away from what you know, society's education is just for show. Step away from the lies, truly, truly open your eyes. The universe is a magnificent place, not understood by the human race. The universe is vast and wide, so many waves for you to ride. The universe is full of wonder, do not allow man's narrow thinking to pull you under. The universe is full of glory, man only sees a small part of the story.

Slowly, slowly we will open your mind, then many wonders will you find. Slowly, slowly we will open your heart, for you to accept this wonderful art. Slowly, slowly you will embrace your fate, to begin this journey, it's not too late. Slowly, slowly will you come to see, that learning magic will set you free.

15th June 2015

More practise must there be, before you will truly see. More practise must you do, before this gift is bestowed on you. More practise must you make, before this gift is yours to take.

Open your mind wide in trust, an open mind is a must. Open your mind wide in love, then you will feel the magic glove. Open your mind wide and free, then this gift you will see.

Practise, practise every day, until you feel the sunshine's ray. Practise, practise every night, until you have the gift of sight. Practise, practise all the time, then I'll teach you the magic rhyme.

Do not question what we do, simply trust me through and through. Trust is needed to reach our goal, trust is the key to opening your soul. Trust in love and trust in me, trust in who you were born to be.

Soon you'll look back on the progress you've made, all your doubts will soon fade, Soon you will see with open eyes, but to get there will take many tries. Soon you'll dance under the stars, and feel the power of Jupiter and Mars. Soon you'll bathe in pools of wisdom, soon you'll have the tools of vision.

So practise, practise every day, soon you'll be ready to have your say. Practise, practise, put your trust in me, then I promise my dear that you will see, for with great knowledge comes great responsibility, this you must master to a tee. With great knowledge comes great love, and a lot of trust from the Lord above. With great knowledge comes great vision, so master this art that you've been given.

16th June 2015

Today you see through evil eyes, today you feel surrounded by lies. Today you put me to the test, today I assure you I will not rest. Today you hold some angst in your heart, a balloon to be released with the throw of a dart. Today you feel some pain in your bones, that carry the sounds of hollowing tones. Today you feel some anger in your skin, anger towards your fellow kin. Today you feel frustration in your head, carrying around weight like a tonne of lead. Today you hold fear in your belly, received through the wires of a very old tele. Today you feel like you want to cry, today you need to understand why.

Today you will see through all the lies, today you will be very wise. Today you will let go of so much pain, today you will dance again in the rain. Today you will release the depths of your soul, today you will be closer to reaching your goal. Today you will have a toxic release, today you will tame the toxic beast. Today you will let go of anger and fear, today you will reconnect with cheer. Today we went very deep, many rewards will you reap. Today you will release so much pain, today will bring about so much gain.

Do not worry about who you are, your engine works like an old car. So much work must be done, to hear that engine return to its hum. So much love must be given, before that car can be driven. So much polish must be used, to take away the years that it was abused. So much knowledge must be restored, before that pedal can be floored. So much work to be done under the bonnet, before it returns to the beauty of a sonnet. So much deeper must we go, for you to truly go with the flow.

Release your fears and anxieties, these are the things that no one else sees. But still are they buried deep and far, with all of the journeys of a very old car. Of course it is your soul I speak of, as you know it's been around the block! Many lives and many masters, some of them absolute disasters. Many lives and many pains, many lives you need to train. Many lives and many heartaches, many scars and many bone breaks. Many lives and many lessons, releasing will take many sessions. Many lives and many hurts, many times pushed in the dirt. Many lives and many humiliations, always fighting for your nations. Many lives and many failures, all adding to your derailment. Many lives and many let downs, many tears and many frowns. Many lives and many leaps, soon you will sow the lessons you've reaped.

No longer can this hold you back, soon you will be back on track. Soon we will hear your engine roar, soon we will see you take flight and soar. Soon we will feel your pedal on the metal, soon you will be ready to go full throttle. Soon in the sun you will sparkle and gleam, like a beautiful Chevy from 1916. Soon your journey can begin, soon we will hear your soul sing. Soon you will see your pain dispelled, soon you will see that your hand I held. Soon you will be light and free, soon you will know how to simply be.

17th June 2015

Love is a word that's often used, love is a word that gets abused. Love is a word that's often heard, love should be as free as a bird. Love is a word that's often said, love keeps people in their head, for love is something that should be felt, rather than a conveyor belt, of actions in one's mind, often making one far from kind. Love is something that should be known, true feelings should be shown.

Often hidden in shrouds of fear, often creating buckets of tears. Love is something that should be treasured, not only used for one's own leisure. Love is something that should be seen, love should be worked at as a team. Love should set your heart on fire, love should take you to the wire. Love should touch a heart so true, love should touch you through and through. Love should make your heart elate, love should not be given in hate.

Oftentimes love is not pure, often used in hope of a cure. Often love is given with conditions, to help with one's own selfish missions. Often love is given in fear, this kind of love doesn't bring about cheer. Often love is not from the heart, often love is the ego's chart. For when love is given from one not whole, often self-love is the goal. When one loves from a place of self-hate, one can't truly open the gate. When one loves from a place of self-loathing, often they behave like a wolf in sheep's clothing.

When one loves from a place of self-worth, one becomes connected with the Earth. When one loves with an open heart, this is always the best place to start. When one loves from a place of truth, their own heart will they soothe. When one loves from a place of self-belief, one will feel such relief.

Love should not be about control, that should not be the ultimate goal. Love should not be about desire, that may turn one into a liar. Love should not be about self-gain, this will bring about misery and pain. Love should not be about the ego, in the act of love this is not your amigo. Love should not be about yourself, this won't bring about spiritual wealth. Love should not be about changing another, ultimately this will make you a terrible lover. Love should not be twisting another's arm, this will only bring about harm. Love should not be given in hate, love like this will change your fate.

Love should be a pleasurable cry, free like the wings of a butterfly. Love should be an honest feeling, this will help to bring about healing. Love should be an open heart, love should be like beautiful art. Love should be given with honesty, love should be a symphony. Love should move you through and through, love should create the power of two. Love should support you all of the way, love should stand with you day by day. Love should help to take away pain, love should make you dance in the rain. Love should hold your hand in darkness, love should hold you up like a harness. Love should make your soul sing, love should much happiness bring.

Love given from one that's not whole, self-validation is their goal. Love given from one who's not secure, into their darkness you will be lured. Love given from one not at peace, seeks to put themselves at ease. Love given from one who's not open, seeks to fix that which is broken. Love given from one who is hurting, their own responsibilities are they shirking, for to give oneself true in love, you must connect with your Lord above. To connect with God is to connect with yourself, this will bring about spiritual wealth, for when you're happy, really deeply and truly, no longer will you treat others cruelly. When you're happy really deeply and truly, no longer will you act way too coolly. For when you're happy really deeply and truly, no longer will your ego be unruly. For when you're happy really deeply and truly, your heart you can give wholly and newly.

The whole human race needs to understand, that falling in love is not a plaster on the hand. So many people give their love, then keep the other caged like a wingless dove. So many people open doors, only to heal their own flaws. So many people others' love take, only to heal their own heartbreak. So many people in love act, only to hide from their own cracks. So many people misbehave, to their ego they are a slave. So many people hurt another, pretending to be the perfect lover. So many people choose another's fate, because they're acting out in hate. So many people live a lie, because inside they do cry. So many people cause such pain, because they seek personal gain.

Reconnect back with your soul, this is always the ultimate goal. This will bring you back to love, this will bring you back to God above. This will help you ease your pain, this will help your mind re-train. This will help your ego rest, this will have you feeling full of zest. This will help you let go of your fears, no longer will you be ruled by tears. This will help you open your heart, this will help you to have a new start. This will help you to be who you are, no longer holding others afar. This will help you to be free, this will help you all to simply be.

18th June 2015

Allow yourself to simply be, I am here to assist thee. Allow yourself to truly flow, I am here to help you go. Allow yourself to simply trust, in this wisdom you have been thrust. Allow yourself to open your mind, know that I will always be kind. Allow yourself to trust in me, then the Kingdom you shall see.

I know you worry what others will say, when it soon becomes the day, for you to stand in your power so strong, for you to know right from wrong. Worry not for you shall shine, and you will open many minds. Worry not for you shall gleam, we shall make quite the team. Worry not for you shall be cherished, as you're standing on the terrace, speaking to all mankind, and leaving the dark days far behind. Worry not for you shall glow, we will put on quite the show. Worry not for you shall shine bright, many hearts will you ignite. Worry not for people will see, just how genuine you will be.

The world is going through a transitional state, the world is moving from a place of hate. The world is vibrating at a different level, no longer in cohorts with the devil. The world is changing at the speed of light, the world is moving to a vibration that's right. The world is changing day by day, many people having their say. The world is opening up to peace, moving to a place where war will cease. The world is ready to be saved, but many people must be brave.

Stand up tall and stand up proud, deliver your message sure and loud. Stand up tall and stand up straight, deliver man away from hate. Stand up tall and stand up strong, deliver man away from wrong. Stand up tall and stand up sure, show man how to be much more. Stand up tall and stand up innately, show man how he's been behaving lately. Stand up tall and stand up strong, soon the time will not be long.

Love thyself, thy neighbour too, in each other do not rue. Love thyself and all around thee, together you will find the key. The key to the Kingdom that is yours, even with all of man's flaws.

Embrace the magic day by day, feel it like the sunshine's ray. Embrace the magic hour by hour, do not be afraid, do not cower. Embrace the magic minute by minute, soon your song you will sing it. Embrace the magic with all of your heart, soon you will master this wonderful art.

19th June 2015

Live in hope and live in trust, positivity is a must. Live in hope and live in light, this will give you the gift of sight. Live in hope and live in laughter, this will bring you your ever after. Live in hope and live in knowledge, this will make your foundations solid. Live in hope and live in truth, this will bring you eternal youth.

Cancer is a serious disease, brought about from the body's dis-ease. Cancer is a serious illness, do not underestimate its realness. Cancer is a serious cause, brought about by synthetic flaws. Cancer is a serious business, propaganda causing dizziness. Cancer is a serious flaw, caused by breaking natural laws.

Synthetic drugs are not the answer, if you really want to cure cancer. Synthetic drugs are not the way, so many people now having their say. Synthetic drugs are not the cure, keep your body natural and pure. Synthetic drugs are not the reason, that some may see another season. Synthetic drugs are not the answer, synthetic drugs bring about cancer.

Return man back to natural laws, this will soon shut the doors, on many of your man-made diseases, filling the pockets of all the big cheeses. Return man back to natural laws, move away from synthetic flaws. Return man back to natural laws, chemical warfare is the cause. Return man back to natural living, back to the gift that God is giving.

Remove the toxins from your food, so many diseases being chewed. Remove the toxins from your water, causing infertility in your daughters. Remove the toxins from your soil, poisoning the land and causing spoil. Remove the toxins from your air, of which your government no longer care. Remove the toxins from your bones, being sprayed by government drones.

Please avoid Monsanto's seed, only planted for man's greed. Please avoid Monsanto's lies, they have been given so many tries. Please avoid Monsanto's madness, their seed that causes destruction and badness. Please avoid Monsanto's darkness, this will leave the Earth in starkness. Please avoid Monsanto's quest, putting your bodies to the test. Please avoid Monsanto's greed, please avoid Monsanto's seed.

Reconnect back with source, feel God's love in full force. Reconnect back with source, reconnect with spiritual laws. Fill your bodies with natural food, no more chemicals to be used. Fill your bodies with fresh air, show your bodies you truly care. Fill your bodies with fresh produce, then cancer you will reduce. Fill your bodies with love and light, get them back to a vibration that's right.

GMO will not feed the world, soon your soil will have spoiled. GMO is toxin poison, which most of you have not chosen. Forced upon you by those with power, whilst you sit around and cower. Taken in by their lies, manipulated by their size. Taken in by their convoluted science, whilst they continue to work in defiance. Taken in by their power, as they spray their chemical shower. Taken in by their greed, as they pollute the Earth with their seed.

You must come together hand in hand, if you wish to save your beautiful land. You must come together, stand as one, together in numbers this can be done. You must come together, side by side, this is the way to change the tide. You must come together tall and strong, this is how you will change what is wrong. You must come together far and wide, for in droves they have lied. You must come together tall and proud, as this destruction cannot be allowed. You must come together near and far, as allowing this madness is simply bizarre. You must come together, all as one, ending the madness can be done.

22nd June 2015

Change is coming on the wind, to wash away all the sins. Change is coming in the rain, to wash away all the pain. Change is coming in the sleet, to help man start a whole new sheet. Change is coming in the clouds, to help man stand tall and proud. Change is coming in the sun, to help man change what he has done.

Restoration will come to your beautiful land, but first you must walk hand in hand. Restoration will come to the Earth, but first man must go through a complete rebirth. Restoration will come to the sea, but first man must learn how to simply be. Restoration will come to the trees, but first man must learn to live with ease. Restoration will come to the sky, but first man must see through all the lies. Restoration will come to the fields, but first man must stop using them for profit and yields. Restoration will come to the sun, but first man must recognise what he has done.

The Earth is dying day by day, to be extinct if man continues this way. The Earth is dying day by day, to be nothing but ashes and erroneous clay. The Earth is dying bit by bit, if man does not his greed quit. The Earth is dying hour by hour, if man does not hear it cower. The Earth is dying bit by bit, if man does not stop this shit.

Toxic fuels and toxic duels, chemical wars and settling old scores. Toxic energy all around, toxic energy shaking the ground. Toxic love and toxic hate, toxicity sealing your fate. Toxic rows and toxic cows, toxic minds and toxic rhymes. Toxic shows and toxic lows, toxic science and toxic defiance. Toxic ups and toxic downs, toxic seeds in the ground. Toxic lies and toxic fries, toxic companies on the rise. Toxic foods affecting your moods, toxic teachings leading to beatings.

Rise together hand in hand, come together and save the land. Rise together, be as one, stand together under the sun. Rise together, change your fate, to save the Earth it's not too late. Rise together, change your ways, move away from the darkened days. Rise together hand in hand, change the fate of your beautiful land.

Not long will it have left, if man continues to leave it bereft. Not much longer will there be, if man continues to pillage the sea. Not long is there now, if man continues to eat the cow. Not long will there be, if man does not heed the warning to turn back to its natural seed. Not much longer will you have, if man does not notice the wrath that he inflicts upon the Earth. The Earth is crying out for you to see, that at one with nature must you be. Return back to natural laws, move away from synthetic flaws, before it becomes too late, to undo that which man will create.

23rd June 2015

Today you feel a little stressed, today you put yourself to the test. Today you have a lot on your mind, to frustration you are resigned. You need to learn to simply be, to ground yourself like an old oak tree. You need to learn to simply know, that these things you can let go. You need to learn to simply see, that all you need is to simply be.

Let go of the stress of your day, get yourself up and put pay to all of the worries on your mind, to yourself just be kind. No matter all the things that you must do, your mind is not allowing the action to come through. Pick yourself up and get on with your day, nothing will be achieved if you continue to lay. Worry not what is on your mind, pick yourself up and you will soon find, that nothing is as bad as it seems, put things into action and let out your screams.

Your mind is too full for anymore lessons, so let's make this one of our shorter sessions. Your mind is too full to embrace your power, so pick yourself up and get in the shower. Wash away the stress of the morning, no need is there for further scorning. Come back tomorrow with a clearer mind, many lessons for you shall you find.

24th June 2015

Madness going on in the world, crazy selfishness being swirled. Madness going on all around, thoughts for others hard to be found. Madness going on in the world, accusations being hurled. Madness going on all around, death and destruction for the sake of a pound. Money is the driving force, through man's veins does it course. Money is the bitter pill, that yourselves you do fill. Money is the driving factor, ploughing over others like a tractor. Money is the evil seed, that causes many a selfish deed.

Too much energy on personal gain, causing others emotional pain. Too much energy on financial rewards, turning your back on the desperate hordes. Too much energy on material worth, turning your back on the beauty of birth. Too much energy on financial lustre, the only energy man seems to muster.

Reconnect back with love, to each other no longer be tough. Reconnect back to source, see how this can change your course. Reconnect back with the heart, from the madness you will depart.

Selfish is as selfish does, people doing things just because. Selfish is as selfish be, closing your eyes and refusing to see. Selfish is as selfish was, money and greed the underlying cause. Selfish is as selfish be, returning to love is the key.

Love is not controlled by greed, love is the desired seed. Love is not controlled by power, love will knock down the darkened tower. Love is not controlled by lust, love is something that you can trust. Love is not controlled by fear, connect in love and you will all be freer. Free from corporate bondage ties, free from all the propaganda and lies. Free from corporate bondage tales, spread through the lands to increase sales. Free from corporate bondage figures, free from corporate gold diggers.

Move away from a need for profit, only lining the top boys' pockets. Move away from a need for riches, whilst allowing others to live in ditches. Move away from a need for money, killing the bees and selling their honey. Move away from a need for material toys, reconnect with natural joys.

Money is a tool of man, to keep you doing all that you can. Money is a man-made illusion, creating greed, fear and confusion. Money is the work of greed, to keep you feeling that there's always a need. Money is the work of the elite, to keep man feeling continuously downbeat. Money is the work of the cruel, to keep themselves in power and rule. Money is the driving force, that keeps man from reconnecting with source.

Love is a much better way, to bring about a brighter day. Love is a much better tool, to make sure that you're fairly ruled. Love is a much better course, to see you returning back to source. Love is a much better canvas, to see you disconnect from the madness. Love is a much better act, to know that you hear truth and fact. Love is a much better path, to bring you together to smile and laugh. Love is a much better way, to bring you back to a brighter day…

24th June 2015 (afternoon)

God is a state of mind. God is a state of peace. God is a state of being. God is a state of seeing. God is a state of love. God is a state of giving. God is a state of action. God is the biggest fraction of each and every one of you, as you feel the love come through. God is a state of acceptance. God is a state of abundance. God is a kind word. God is the day that has dawned. God is a feeling of peace. God is a feeling of ease. God is the love of a mother. God is a new born brother. God is love so true. God is me and you. God is everywhere. God is a soul laid bare. God is everyone. God is the light that is shone. God is me and you. God is us through and through.

God is not to be feared, God should never be revered. God is not a man of malice, drinking out of a golden chalice. God is not a bearded shroud, sitting high on a pure white cloud. God is not any one thing, God is simply everything.

God is here and God is there, God can be felt in the air. God is here and God is there, God can be felt everywhere. Open your minds to what God is, no longer get yourselves in a tizz. All this talk of a man of wrath, sometimes I think you're having a laugh! God is love and God is light, but sometimes God may give you a fright.

On your learning curve you are, to twinkle like a beautiful star. Experiencing yourselves as matter, illusions of self you will soon shatter. God will help you find yourself, God will help your spiritual wealth. God will shine in everything that you do, even something as simple as tying your shoe. God will whisper in your ear, God will help to take away fear, but first you must listen to that voice, the one in your head that gives you a choice. First you must open up your heart, to feel God's love and to be smart.

God is love and God is fear, God is pain and God is cheer. God is dark and God is light, God is wrong and God is right. God is me and God is you, God is in everything that we do.

The choice is yours what path you choose, but live in fear and yourself you will lose. The choice is yours what decisions you make, but live in hate and yourself you will break. The choice is yours in what way you connect, there are many ways that you can select, but listen to what your soul says, man's scriptures are only a guess. Listen to what your soul cries, see through man's age old lies. Listen to what your soul needs, listen to it then plant the seeds. Listen to what your soul desires, God's love will not be biased. Listen to what your soul requires, as your souls will never be liars.

Connect with yourself and connect with God, give yourself a little prod. Connect with yourself, connect with your soul, to experience yourself is the ultimate goal. Connect with yourself, connect with your beauty, this is part of your karmic duty. Connect with yourself, connect with love, give yourself a great big shove. Connect with yourself, connect with others, connect with your holy band of brothers. Open your heart and let your soul be laid bare, in each other's dreams you will share. Open your heart and open your mind, then God you are sure to find.

3rd July 2015

Trust is the name of the game, trust will bring about fortune and fame. I know these things are not what you seek, but still you must have a platform to speak. I know you will give the money away, I know you don't want to be paid to have your say. But still these things will come to you, because you're genuine through and through. Still these things will come your way, as it is how you will have your say.

The orphanage that you wish to build, with your earnings it will be filled. The school that you wish to grow, because of you people will show. The children that you wish to help, out of the darkness they will delve. The system that you wish to implement, soon it will start to make a dent, in the current systems held, that to move forward must be shelled.

You already know what must be done, current systems must be shunned. You already know a better way, soon you will be able to have your say. Bring those children back to love, keep them connected with the Lord above. Help those children to understand, that with each other they walk hand in hand. Help those children to live from their soul, help them to know it's the ultimate goal. Help those children to know who they are, help them to know they don't have to look far. Help them to stay connected with self, help them to know themselves deep in their cells. Help those children to stay true to love, into their ego do not shove. Help those children to find their gifts, for these are the children that will heal the rifts.

Very special children will be in your care, these are the children who will truly dare, to bare their souls and gifts to the world, the children whose voices need to be heard. These are the children who will stand in love, strong in the power of God above. These are the children who will speak from their heart, because they have had the best possible start.

Never from ego will they act, because their true selves will never be cracked. Never from ego will they be, because from their souls they will truly see. Never from ego will they speak, because they know that ego is weak. Never from ego will they wonder, because no one will ever steal their thunder. Never from ego will they behave, because their true selves you will save.

Do not worry about how to do it, you already know that you can get through it. Do not worry about where to go, you already know in time we will show. Do not worry about where to be, in time you will be ready to see. Do not worry about what to do, soon the tools will be available to you.

People gather from far and wide, they will be there for the ride. People come from here and there, in your task they will share. People come from around the world, soon the magic will be twirled. People will come to help you, together you will know what to do.

Until then hold the love in your heart, soon enough you will be ready to start. Until then see with open eyes, continue to see through the lies. Until then speak with a true voice, help people to see that they have a choice. Until then stand in your power so strong, help man to see right from wrong.

5th July 2015

Love is as love does, fear is as fear be. Open up your heart and see, how you're truly meant to be. Love is as love does, love shows us the true us. Fear is as fear be, fear holds us in captivity. Love is as love does, love gives us all a buzz. Fear is as fear be, only negativity will we see.

Open up your heart in love, on this matter I'll continue to shove. Love is the only way, to bring about a better day. Love is the only truth, love even bitter hearts soothe. Love is the only matter, fear and contempt will it shatter. Love is the only act, to help the world change its tact. Love is the only voice, to give you all a better choice.

Live in love and live in hope, important changes will this provoke. Live in love and live in glory, help the world rewrite its story. Live in love and live in joy, reconnect man with boy. Live in love and live in laughter, live happily ever after.

The world has lived in fear for years, surrounded by each other's tears. The world has lived in fear forever, man being pushed to the end of his tether. The world has lived in fear for so long, man not knowing right from wrong. The world has lived in fear for always, lost in fear's smoggy haze.

Fear creates a world of pain, keeps man locked up in his chain. Fear creates a world of worry, everyone in such a hurry. Fear creates a world of hate, fear is a heavy trait. Fear creates a world of danger, even for the baby in the manger. Fear creates a world of doubt, only hearing the loudest shout. Fear creates a world of terror, man living his life in error. Fear creates broken man, stopping him from being all that he can.

Do not be afraid of change, at first it may seem a little strange, but as you open your heart to beauty, you'll start to recognise your only duty. Duty is not to make ends meet, only allowing the occasional treat. Duty is not to toe the line, trying to avoid a heavy fine. Duty is not to bow your head in shame, in the way that you've been trained. Duty is not to conform to others, being the same as all your brothers. Duty is not to close your mind, to all of the magic that you could find.

Duty is to be true, to you, yourself and only you. Duty is to know yourself fully, no longer living your life dully. Duty is to know who you are, to recognise you're a twinkling star. Duty is to trust your soul, allow it to lead you to your goal. Duty is to express your emotions, let them flood with the power of the oceans. Duty is to take life's ride, your true self never hide. Duty is to open your eyes, duty is to see through the lies.

Treat others with love and kindness, to others' needs do not show blindness. Treat others with love and respect, your actions to others should be checked, but never, ever neglect yourself, don't put your dreams on the shelf. Never, ever ignore your needs, ignoring needs plants bad seeds. Never ever forget your passion, happiness is not on ration. Never, ever forget your beauty, knowing yourself is your duty.

Being the source of another's happiness never works, this turns man into jerks. Asking another to make you whole, this will soon take its toll. Relying on another to seal your fate, this turns love into hate. Putting your life in another's hand, soon you'll be stepping in sinking sand. Asking another to choose your path, soon for them you will only feel wrath. Asking another to lead the way, will move you away from the sunshine's ray. Expecting another to be your aid, soon your soul's sparkle will fade.

Always follow your own path, avoid feeling your own wrath. Always follow your own way, always listen to what your soul has to say. Always treat yourself with love, handle with care, don't push and shove. Always speak from your heart, this is always the best place to start. See what happens when you do, see how your dreams come to you. See what happens when you try, life is no longer barren and dry. See what happens when you connect, when your soul you do respect. See what happens when you try, spread your wings and begin to fly. See what happens when you do, see how much wonder comes to you.

6th July 2015

Intuition is your friend, to it your time you should lend. Intuition is your pal, in its hands soon you shall. Intuition is your truth, listen to it and have the proof. Intuition is your right, intuition is the gift of sight.

You are all born with this gift, but of its existence you seem to be miffed. You are all born with this crown, but its wise words you seem to drown. You are all born with this armour, but instead you prefer to be wrapped in the drama. The drama of the ego's plight, thinking ego's always right. The drama of the ego's goal, to keep you from connecting with your soul.

Trust in the information that comes, move aside the irrelevant sums. Trust in the information you get, guaranteed that it's a safe bet. Trust in the information that shows, getting stronger as your trust grows. Trust in the information that opens, intuition should have your full focus.

Move away from what you've been taught, much information heavily bought. Move away from what you have seen, intuition buried since you were a teen. Move away from what you were shown, learn to feel and think on your own. Move away from what you have known, things are different from what you've been shown.

The universe is a great big light, offering man the gift of sight. The universe is a great big bang, so many songs still to be sang. The universe holds infinite wisdom, so much to show you if you would listen. The universe is a place full of promise, wanting to connect with a heart that is honest. The universe is a magical place, so much mystery for you to embrace. The universe is a magnificent tool, to block it out you must be a fool.

Open to the power of creative thought, a magical gift that has been thwart. Open to the power of creative ways, an easy way to change your days. Open to the power of creative beauty, the way to live your karmic duty. Open to the power of creative desire, throw negativity into the fire. Open to the power of creative minds, embrace the magic that you shall find. Open to the power of creative thought, release the negativity that you have been taught.

You create your lives with your minds, negativity finds you in all kinds of binds. You create your lives with your thoughts, negativity tying you all in knots. You create your lives with your dreams, negativity ripping at the seams. You create your lives with your words, negativity often the tendency heard.

Break away from society's chains, chains keeping you all in pain. Break away from society's fears, fears that lead to too many tears. Break away from society's trappings, trappings holding you in negativity's wrappings. Break away from society's teachings, teachings taught from misplaced preachings. Break away from society's chains, no longer living under its constraints.

Reconnect back to source, feel the universe in full force. Reconnect back to self, get back to mental health. Reconnect back to love, feel the magic from above. Reconnect back to beauty, understand your karmic duty. Reconnect back to source, no longer feel guilt and remorse. Reconnect back to source, reconnect with spiritual laws. Reconnect back to source, get man back to his natural course.

7th July 2015

Reaction is the law of attraction, reaction reduces your light by a fraction. Reaction sees your brains combust, reaction is a trait of lust. Reaction is an angry flaw, reaction sees you slamming doors. Reaction is a fit of fear, reaction sees you reduced to tears. Reaction is the devil's* deed, reaction is the devil's seed.

To learn to live in harmony, first you must learn to simply be. To learn to live without fear, from your heart you must be freer. To learn to live without reaction, your soul's dreams you must put into action. To learn to live with your brothers, first you must learn to accept one another.

You all react in different ways, reactions changing the flow of your days. You all react to different things, much confusion does this bring. You all react to different flaws, often not knowing what is the cause. You all react to different words, not knowing who said what first. You all react to different reasons, changing your minds with the seasons. You all react to different pain, for this fear is always to blame.

Fear comes in many ways, fear constricts you throughout your days. Fear comes in many forms, shaking you up and creating storms. Fear comes in many disguises, in many shapes and in many sizes. Fear comes from a heart, that was filled with fear from the start. Fear comes from a place, where trust was removed without a trace. Fear comes from external forces, different people of different courses. Fear comes from all your lives, from all the pain and all the lies. Fear comes from society's teachings, from your soul they are leeching. Fear comes in many ways, to create anxiety in your days.

Release this torture from your soul, reconnect with your ultimate goal. Release this fear from your heart, rediscover the gift of your art. Release this darkness from your journey, remove yourself from your gurney. Release these shackles from your feet, no longer allow it to keep you downbeat. Release the anger from your mind, to each other be nothing but kind.

Recognise society's flaws, understand that this is the cause. Recognise the feeling of fear, keep your mind much more clear. Recognise all of the pain, caused by society's inflicted shame. Recognise this feeling inside, as your true self you do hide. Recognise the swallowed feeling, of your anger hitting the ceiling. Recognise your downtrodden soul, restrained from reaching its ultimate goal. Recognise your hands are tied, easily released if only you tried.

If every one of you lived from your heart, this would bring about a whole new start. If every one of you lived from your soul, this would change society's role. If every one of you lived with ease, this would help to melt the freeze. If every one of you lived with joy, no longer would you be society's toy. If every one of you spoke your truth, no one would ever ask for proof. If every one of you lived in love, no longer would people push and shove. If every one of you stood in your power, no longer would anyone fear and cower. If every one of you embraced each other, no longer would you have need to fear one another.

Open up your heart in strength, for this go to any length. Open up your heart in beauty, reconnect with your karmic duty. Open up your heart in ease, to your soul don't be a tease. Open up your heart to laughter, see how you get your ever after. Open up your heart to others, stand in love with your band of brothers. Open up your heart to love, open up to God above.

*Is the devil real is the question you ask, again you have given me quite the task. The devil is not a man with horns, the devil is all of man's sharp thorns. In everything there is shadow and light, this is how man learns to get things right. In everyone there is good and bad, this is how man learns to be happy and sad. In everyone there is joy and pain, this is how man learns to dance in the rain. In everyone there is evil and kindness, this is how man learns to see through the blindness. In everyone there is bitterness and love, this is how man learns to connect with the Lord above.

The time is now to push evil away, no longer room for evil to stay. The time is now to connect with truth, pushing away all that's uncouth. The time is now to bring love back, to reconnect with the beauty you lack. The time is now to banish fear, to wipe away the final tear. The time is now to let love in, washing away every sin. The time is now to change your ways, putting behind you the difficult days. The time is now to change your course, to do this simply connect with source.

8th July 2015

The human mind is a spurious tool, often making man a fool. The human mind is of spurious nature, storing all of your learned behaviour. The human mind is a spurious weapon, sending you into the depths of depression. The human mind is a spurious function, man living in total dysfunction. The human mind is a spurious notion, manipulated by man's devotion. The human mind is a spurious act, desperately trying to grab at the facts. The human mind is a spurious tissue, often creating many an issue.

Man lives deeply in his mind, to his soul often blind. Man lives deeply in his head, intuition to him is dead. Man lives deeply in his brain, caught up in all his shame. Man lives deeply in his ego, never allowing the soul to have a free go. Man lives deeply in his grey matter, illusions of self, hard to shatter.

Man needs to learn to feel, only then will he know what's real. Man needs to learn to open, only then will he fix what's broken. Man needs to learn to hear, only then will he turn from fear. Man needs to learn to know, recognising tales of show. Man needs to learn to be, through the charades he will see. Man needs to learn to search, answers won't be found in church. Man needs to learn to trust, in himself this is a must. Man needs to learn live, from his heart and truly forgive.

Forgive each other for the pain, brought about by personal gain. Forgive each other for the rifts, brought about by all the myths. Forgive each other for the darkness, live from the heart there will no longer be starkness. Forgive each other for the madness, overblown ego's causing sadness. Forgive each other for the hurt, kicking each other to the dirt. Forgive each other for the hate, know that your neighbour is your mate. Forgive each other for the torture, brought about by spiritual disorder. Forgive each other for the pain, forgive yourselves your personal shame.

No longer be taken in by the lies, lies coming in constant supplies. No longer be taken in by the greed, man's deeply planted seed. No longer be taken in by manipulation, coming through your TV stations. No longer be taken in by the noise, coming from the mouths of the world's top boys. No longer be taken in by the creations, of the lobbying corporations. No longer be taken in by false science, results manipulated in defiance. No longer be taken in by technology's rise, too much advancement is far from wise. No longer be taken in by the lies, often coming in incredible disguise.

Feel your way through the madness, steer yourselves away from sadness. Feel your way through the red tape, know your soul can create an escape. Feel your way through the darkness, open up to catharsis. Feel your way through the crowds, see through all the thick clouds. Feel your way to the truth, what you feel won't need any proof. Feel your way to the answers, know that society's full of chancers. Feel your way out of your mind, to your soul no longer be blind.

9th July 2015

As all the flowers come to bloom, their colours help to wash away gloom. As all the trees come to pass, we see the greenness of the grass. As all the birds make their call, we know that it will soon be fall. As all the moles dig their holes, playing out natures roles. As all the fish swim around, making only a gentle sound. As all the cattle roam the fields, being used for profit and yields. As all the monkeys swing from the trees, we slowly kill off all the bees. As all the crabs walk through the sand, we slowly kill off all the land. As all the insects fly through the air, we pollute it without a care. As all the wildlife roam the forests, to ourselves we are not being honest. As all the wildlife slowly dies, we let it happen with closed eyes.

Soon the day will come to pass, where we are left on our ass. Soon the day will come to call, when summer doesn't turn to fall. Soon the day will come to be, where the land is covered by sea. Soon the day will come to know, where the land is covered in snow. Soon the day will come to play, when the Earth can't feel the sunshine's ray. Soon the day will come to matter, when the core of the Earth will shatter.

We need to change our selfish ways, rushing around in a hurried haze. We need to change our selfish means, messing around with synthetic genes. We need to change our selfish manners, polluting ourselves with all types of cancers. We need to change our selfish demeanours, taking each other to the cleaners. We need to change our selfish acts, trusting in twisted facts. We need to change our selfish lives, stabbing others' backs with knives. We need to change our selfish ways, to avoid coming to darker days.

Soon the core of the Earth will crack, once it does there is no turning back. Soon the core of the Earth will shatter, leaving behind nothing but matter. Soon the core of the Earth will bleed, with the poison of Monsanto's seed. Soon the core of the Earth will die, no longer able to take the lies. Soon the core of the Earth will shift, from its axis it will lift. Soon the core of the Earth will move, taking the planet out of its groove. Soon the core of the Earth will die, to life as we know it we can kiss goodbye.

It's not too late to change this fate, simply turn your back on hate. It's not too late to change this seed, move away from corporate greed. It's not too late to change this goal, simply connect to your soul. It's not too late to change this disaster, all of your gifts simply master. It's not too late to change this feeling, change the things that leave you reeling. It's not too late to change Earth's plight, but corporate greed you must fight. It's not too late to change this motion, coming together in love is the potion.

Come together hand in hand, work in harmony with the land. Come together day by day, connect to your heart and have your say. Come together all as one, know that it can be done. Come together near and far, together we can raise the bar. Come together all as one, from this challenge do not run.

10th July 2015

Love to hate and hate to love, love to play way too rough. Love to hate and hate to love, love to play push and shove. Love to hate and hate to love, love to teach with love that's tough. Love to hate and hate to love, love to hate way too much.

Hatred comes from darkened hearts, those around you playing their parts. Hatred comes from darkened lives, oblivious to the beautiful skies. Hatred comes from darkened nights, always eager for a fight. Hatred comes from darkened places, conveyor belts of life's rat races. Hatred comes from darkened feelings, disconnected from life's true meaning. Hatred comes from darkened souls, never achieving their intended goals.

Darkened seeds infecting the soul, darkened seeds taking their toll. Darkened seeds bringing you down, keeping you in your home town. Darkened seeds breeding fear, leading to angry tears. Darkened seeds breeding contempt, anger to others often sent. Darkened seeds growing like moss, never truly connecting to loss. Darkened seeds breaking you down, always wearing your smile like a frown. Darkened seeds causing you pain, making you feel like you're insane. Darkened seeds breaking hearts, filling up your shopping carts, with the food that makes you sick, it's all that's left that makes you tick.

Negativity feeds your soul, distracts you from your desired goal. Negativity feeds your lives, slowly bringing you out in hives. Negativity brings you down, rarely connecting to your inner clown. Negativity feeds your days, oblivious of another way. Negativity drowns you out, making you want to kick and shout.

Disconnection breeds contempt, on this course you are hell-bent. Disconnection turns to anger, to this emotion you often pander. Disconnection turns to hurt, leading to feelings of inert. Disconnection turns to pain, caught up in material chains. Disconnection turns to distance, always causing you such resistance. Disconnection affects your health, leading you away from spiritual wealth.

Love is the only way, to bring about a brighter day. Love is the only feeling, that will see you reaching for the ceiling. Love is the only goal, to make you feel complete and whole. Love is the only answer, to find your dreams a little faster. Love is the only step, to stop you feeling deeply inept. Love is the only path, to stop you feeling shy and daft. Love is the only reason, to bring about another season.

13th July 2015

Tired hearts and tired minds, often missing all the signs. Tired hearts and tired minds, getting yourselves in all kinds of binds. Tired hearts and tired minds, often leaving logic behind.

So much stress and so much worry, rushing around in such a hurry. So much stress and so much woe, can't decide which way to go. So much stress and so much drama, often creating much more karma. So much stress and so much fear, the right path never clear.

Take time to meditate, this will connect you with your fate. Take time to sit in silence, this will steer you away from violence. Take time to be with yourself, this will improve your mental health. Take time to see your fears, this will help to relinquish tears. Take time to open up, drink from the spiritual cup. Take time to know your truth, of yourself you do not need proof. Take time to seal your fate, for this journey it's never too late.

Gifted beings you all are, powerful as a twinkling star. Gifted beings you all be, but often fear doesn't allow you to see. Gifted beings you all make, the power is there for you all to take. Gifted beings you all know, but your ego drags you all so low. Gifted beings you all start, until you move away from your heart.

Look inside for your dreams, it's not as hard as it seems. Look inside for your wisdom, no longer be society's victim. Look inside for your knowledge, you'll learn more there than you will in college. Look inside for your answers, don't put faith in external chancers. Look inside for your freedom, always follow your internal beacon. Look inside for your faith, in your wisdom you will bathe. Look inside for yourself, soon you will find your spiritual wealth.

Take time from your busy day, listen to what your soul has to say. Take time from your busy morning, appreciate the new day that's dawning. Take time from your busy night, connect with yourself and regain sight. Take time from your busy schedule, take yourself to another level. Take time from your busy week, then you will find what you seek. Take time from your busy lives, see how you grow and thrive.

Trapped in the rat race, spinning on the wheel at society's pace. Trapped in society's tool, making you feel like a fool. Trapped in society's creation, never time to feel elation. Trapped in society's making, living lives that you are faking. Trapped in society's structure, waiting for your heart to rupture. Trapped in society's ways, never questioning how you fill your days.

Life is a precious jewel, to waste it you would be a fool. Life is a precious gift, it's not too late to make a shift. Life is a precious stone, always working your fingers to the bone. Life is a precious right, reconnect with your gift of sight. Life is a precious moment, you can't get back what has been stolen. Life is a precious means, there's always time to change the scenes. Life is a precious act, it's not too late to change your tack.

14th July 2015

Gifted people walk the Earth, to help with its complete rebirth. Gifted people walk this plane, to others' minds help retrain. Gifted people walk the planet, to move away from a life that's manic. Gifted people walk the streets, flushing out all the cheats. Gifted people walk the roads, seeing through society's codes. Gifted people walk the lanes, moving people out of their brains. Gifted people are here in droves, walking around in normal clothes.

The time is now to flush them out, to be heard they must shout. The time is now to all connect, of your missions do not neglect. The time is now to stand as one, this is how God's will shall be done. The time is now to realign, open your eyes and see the sign. The time is now to stand so tall, flat on your face you will not fall. The time is now to have your voice, help man to see there's always a choice. The time is now to be as one, responsibilities do not shun.

Walk together in your power, walk away from a taste that's sour. Walk together in your strength, strong in numbers the world's length. Walk together in your passion, put your knowledge into action. Walk together in your hoards, let your wisdom be your swords. Walk together strong as one, this is how God's will shall be done.

15th July 2015

Cluttered hearts and cluttered minds, peace and quiet hard to find. Cluttered hearts and cluttered minds, intuition left behind. Cluttered hearts and cluttered heads, often filled with worry and dread. Cluttered hearts and cluttered voices, often leading to many bad choices. Cluttered hearts and cluttered motives, intuition never noticed. Cluttered hearts and cluttered souls, living out empty roles.

Taking time for yourself, will lead to better mental health. Taking time for your dreams, is not as hard as it seems. Taking time to write your story, will never be an act that's corny. Taking time to find your way, something you can start today. Taking time to find your path, doesn't need a compass and map. Taking time to find your route, connect to yourself before you shoot. Taking time to lay your plans, with your soul you're in good hands.

In your soul you hold the key, to be everything that you want to be. In your soul you hold the knowledge, simply wipe away the blockage. In your soul you hold the wisdom, realign with your vision. In your soul you hold the answers, open the gate to your life enhancers. In your soul you hold it all, open your mind and hear its call.

Move away from your head, soon you will release a weight of lead. Move away from your mind, soon to yourself you will start to be kind. Move away from your brain, soon you will release misery and pain. Move away from your ego, ego's nothing more than a placebo. Move away from your mind, leave fear and worry behind.

16th July 2015

Worry, worry on your mind, worry, worry all the time. Worry, worry throughout your days, worry causing quite a haze. Worry, worry all the time, mind too foggy for you to shine. Worry, worry through your lives, worry is how the ego thrives.

Negativity getting you down, negativity causing a frown. Negativity pulling you under, keeping you all in your slumber. Negativity darkening your days, negativity never pays. Negativity creates your lives, negativity cuts your size. Negativity drowns you out, negativity creates a drought. Negativity diminishes your light, no longer sparkling quite so bright. Negativity keeps your hands tied, even when you feel like you have tried. Negativity darkens your path, living the creation of your own wrath. Negativity is your foe, only creating a life of woe.

It's time to look for the flickering light, even in darkness it's still in sight. It's time to look for the flickering beam, even in tough times it can be seen. It's time to look for the flickering bulb, it's time for the darkness to be culled. It's time to look for the flickering motion, the lighthouse in the great big ocean. It's time to look for the flickering map, this will get you back on track.

Into the light must you step, no longer feeling out of depth. Into the light must you go, negativity must you throw. Into the light must you be, of negativity it's time to be free. Into the light must you run, into a life that's much more fun. Into the light must you stand, negativity to be banned.

You choose what path you want to follow, swim with the fish or fly with the swallow. You choose what path you want to make, the world is yours for you to take. You choose what path you want to sow, flying high or sailing low. You choose what path you want to see, tied in chains or roaming free. You choose what path you want to know, staying put or continuing to grow. You choose what path you want to take, understand this for your own sake.

Step by step you can change your ways, move away from negativity's haze. Step by step you can change your choices, listen to your inner voices. Step by step you can change your story, bring it back to one of glory. Step by step you can change your decisions, open yourself to brighter visions. Step by step you can change your course, moving forward with the power of a horse. Step by step you can change your lives, go ahead, give it a try.

17th July 2015

The secret to a still mind, to not getting caught in a bind, is to just simply be, and let go of your worry. I know it seems hard to do, but to yourself just be true. I know it seems hard to be, but live from your heart and your mind will be free. I know it seems hard to change, at first it will seem a little strange, but slowly move away from your head, letting go of the endless thread, of thoughts swirling in your mind, to chaos you are resigned. Let go of the endless stream, of thoughts making you want to scream. Let go of the endless torture, that you still allow to haunt you. Let go of the endless noise, that makes you often lose your poise. Let go of the endless drama, used as your protective armour.

Take time to be you, do the things that you want to do. Take time to be who you are, soon you will see you have come so far. Take time to love yourself, into your soul take time to delve. Take time to be wise, strip away your disguise. Take time to be free, then your true self you will see.

You all need to strip away, the demeanour that's in full play. You all need to connect to self, put ego on the shelf. You all need to hear your soul, to get you back to a place that's whole. You all need to love each other, your true selves do not smother. You all need to find your way, to bring about a better day.

Facts and figures in your head, carried around like a lump of lead. Facts and figures in your mind, to the truth you are all blind. Facts and figures in your brain, the truth of the matter you do feign. Facts and figures in your genes, without even knowing exactly what it means. Facts and figures, all you know, the way that man has continued to grow. Facts and figures bogging you down, in these figures you will drown. Facts and figures blinding your mind, truth and lies have become entwined.

Connect to self and see the truth, your perception will this move. Connect to self and see the way, get yourself back to play. Connect to truth and see the shift, see how this will heal the rift. Connect to self and be assured, that into darkness you won't be lured. Connect to self and understand, you are connected to the land. Connect to self and come to know, society's rules are just for show. Connect to self and be free, then the truth you will see.

18th July 2015

Shattered dreams and scattered thoughts, thoughts taking you far off course. Shattered dreams and scattered heads, heads keeping you living in dread. Shattered dreams and scattered minds, minds keeping you all enshrined. Shattered dreams and scattered lives, illusions of a life that thrives.

Caught up in material toys, sucking the life from natural joys. Caught up in material worth, bleeding the resources of the Earth. Caught up in material wealth, leading you all to much ill health. Caught up in material lives, even though happiness this deprives.

Walk in nature, see its beauty, away from an office that's grey and gloomy. Walk in nature, see the flowers in bloom, smell the scent of their sweet perfume. Walk in nature, feel its power, dance in nature's natural shower. Walk in nature, connect to the Earth, maybe even learn to surf. Walk in nature, be as one, turn your face to the sun. Walk in nature, take it in, listen to the birds that sing. Walk in nature, embrace its charms, welcome it with open arms.

Through these journeys you will find, that your mind you leave behind. Through these journeys you will see, that with nature you can simply be. Through these journeys you will know, material worth is just for show. Through these journeys you will embrace, connecting to yourself with ease and grace. Through these journeys you will start, to live your life with an open heart. Through these journeys you will go, moving into nature's flow. Through these journeys you will see, living from the heart is the way to be.

Take time to appreciate, even when you're running late. Take time to take it all in, even when your time's spread thin. Take time to embrace life, even when you are in strife. Take time to open your arms, feel the power of life's charms. Take time to love yourself, take your dreams from the shelf. Take time to feel your beauty, dance around and shake your bootie. Take time to feel your love, even when life is rough. Take time to feel your power, break down negativity's tower.

19th July 2015

So much hatred all around, hatred seeping through the ground. So much hatred in your bones, in the sound of tortured moans. So much hatred in the air, hurting others without a care. So much hatred everywhere, love and forgiveness very rare.

Soldiers going off on tour, to fight another manmade war. Soldiers going to do their duty, to stop the world from being unruly. Soldiers going off on tour, because their country wants much more. Soldiers going to do their duty, eating away at their inner beauty. Soldiers going off on tour, to help to settle their country's score. Soldiers going to do their duty, often inflicting a lot of cruelty. Soldiers going off on tour, so much pain do they endure.

Fighting for misguided reasons, often touring for many seasons. Fighting for misguided truths, easily manipulated when they are youths. Fighting for misguided acts, never given all the facts. Fighting for their country's pride, for the homeland that they reside. Fighting for a better day, believing this is the only way. Fighting for the love of their nation, as they bravely take their station.

Buying into the world's divide, another way has not been tried. Buying into the world's divide, buying into their country's pride. Buying into the world's divide, for this reason so many have died. Buying into the world's divide, instead of listening to their internal guide. Buying into the world's divide, propaganda spread worldwide.

Wars are often fought for greed, under the pretence of another need. Wars are often fought for power, whilst those seeking it stay safe in their tower. Wars are often fought for glory, under the pretence of another story. Wars are often fought for oil, for who has the right to the soil. Wars are often fought for greed, but planted is a different seed.

Take away the invisible lines, that determine where one resides. Take away the invisible ceilings, that lead to many selfish dealings. Take away the invisible walls, see how separation falls. Take away the invisible doors, that lead to all the unjust wars. Take away the invisible habits, that cause destruction to the planet. Take away the invisible force, that leaves you feeling such remorse.

Recognise you are all one, no longer point and shoot the gun. Recognise you're all God's children, to each other start to listen. Recognise you're all from source, each other's will do not force. Recognise you all have beauty, loving each other is your duty. Recognise you are all one, working together can be done.

Feel your way through the lies, to war these lies can give rise. Feel your way through the drama, find your way to a place that's calmer. Feel your way through the truths, see how hatred this soon soothes. Feel your way through closed doors, see how this puts an end to wars.

20th July 2015

Liars, cheats, murderers and thieves, seemingly living their lives with ease. Rapists, gangsters, animal and wife beaters, living their lives as their victim's teeters. Always looking over their shoulder, wondering if they'll have a chance to grow older. Living their lives from a place of hate, pent up feelings of being innate. Living their lives from a place of fear, their own pain they do not hear. Living their lives from a place of inertia, close to exploding with the pressure. Living their lives from a place of dread, listening to the darkness in their head.

Lost are these tortured souls, unable to connect with their desired goals. Lost are these tortured beings, from the madness they need freeing. Lost are these tortured men, can't get out of their darkened den. Lost are these tortured minds, further into darkness themselves they find.

You all hold the key in your heart, to help them find a brand new start. You all hold the key in your soul, to help them reconnect with their goal. You all hold the key in your voices, to help them to make better choices. You all hold the key in your arms, to help them find their own true charms. You all hold the key in your love, to help them connect with God above.

Throwing away the key is not the answer, I know many think it should be harsher. Throwing away the key is not the way, for them their blackened heart betray. Throwing away the key will not change their fate, to move away from darkness it's not too late.

Turn ye not your back in anger, further will their darkness fracture. Turn ye not your back in hate, this will only enhance their trait. Turn ye not your back in loathing, the capital punishment that you're imposing. Turn ye not your back in fear, hatred's ugly head will rear. Turn ye not your back in sadness, this will only encourage their badness.

Love is the only way, to allow a soul to have its say. Love is the only form, to put together a soul that's torn. Love is the only feeling, to bring about spiritual healing. Love is the only answer, to move away from a soul's disaster. Love is the only reason, to move away from lies and treason. Love is the only goal, to make a broken soul whole.

Work with people day by day, allow that soul to have its say. Work with people in dark places, teach them to own their disgraces. Work with people in much pain, from this you all have so much to gain. Work with people in much anger, teach them a more gentle manner. Work with people who need much love, teach them not to push and shove. Work with people who need support, to break away from what they're taught. Work with people, it's in your power, to no longer at them glower. Work with people to be free, of a darkened soul's agony.

21st July 2015

Twisted hearts and twisted minds, twisted logic, twisted finds. Twisted hearts and twisted minds, leaving compassion far behind. Twisted hearts and twisted minds, to this logic you're all resigned.

Bowing down to Monsanto's greed, trusting when they say there's a need. Bowing down to Monsanto's logic, when money is their only object. Bowing down to Monsanto's lies, even when they've polluted the skies. Bowing down to Monsanto's greed, happily eating their poisoned seed.

Trusting in their fabricated research, whilst Agent Orange you besmirch. Trusting in their lobbying tactics, coming at you from all demographics. Trusting in their deadly poisons, early deaths you all have chosen. Trusting in their deadly ways, as their lies they use to phase. Trusting in scientists on their payroll, world domination is their goal.

Control the seed, control the world, treat the masses as a herd. Control the seed, control the planet, even though these actions will damn it. Control the seed, control the Earth, bleed it for everything it's worth. Control the seed, control the people, manipulate with all that's evil. Control the seed, control the money, a situation that's not even funny.

You have to move away from this greed, for this seed there is no need. You have to move away from this violence, toxic seeds working in defiance. You have to move away from this madness, all it will cause is misery and sadness. You have to move away from this seed, you have to recognise Monsanto's greed.

Listen to what your heart says, soon you will feel full of dread. Listen to where your heart takes you, soon this madness you will see through. Listen to what your heart screams, twisted science not what it seems. Listen to what your heart knows, causing destruction wherever it goes. Listen to what your heart demands, toxic poison destroying the lands. Listen to what your heart beseeches, so many laws Monsanto breeches.

Recognise all the flaws, see the disaster this will cause. Recognise all the issues, as it damages your internal tissues. Recognise all the pieces, into your organs this seed leeches. Recognise all the holes, in Monsanto's supposed goals. Recognise all the lies, as your body slowly dies. Recognise all the evil, don't forget you still have free will. Recognise the manipulation, as they bury the litigation. Recognise Monsanto's past, Agent Orange has been downcast.

Still you trust all their lies, despite the evils of days gone by. Still you trust all the fabrication, despite the damage done to many nations. Still you trust all the propaganda, to twisted logic you all pander. Still you trust in your leaders, even though they are money bleeders. Still you trust in the lies, falling for their cloaked disguise.

Follow the money and you will know, that their words are just for show. Follow the money and you will see, the darkness of the reality. Follow the money and you will make, that their persona is nothing but fake. Follow the money and you will believe, that your life this seed will thieve. Follow the money and you will become, from this seed you will quickly run. Follow the money and you will know, that this seed has to go.

Polluted becomes your body and mind, to you this seed will not be kind. Polluted becomes the Earth and the sky, as you are taken in by the lie. Polluted becomes the Earth's very core, on this seed shut the door. Polluted becomes the wind and the rain, from this seed you have nothing to gain. Polluted becomes all that you know, as the Earth's natural seed can no longer grow.

22nd July 2015

Cancer in your water pipes, cancer always in your sight. Cancer in the food you eat, a disease that will be hard to beat. Cancer in the clothes you wear, natural material very rare. Cancer in the cars you drive, more ingrained the more you strive. Cancer in the air you breathe, from your bodies it will not leave. Cancer in the drugs you take, better they will not you make.

Cancer is a serious disease, bringing man to his knees. Cancer is a serious business, the next generation you will ask forgiveness. Cancer is a serious fate, turn things around before it's too late.

Move away from factory farming, cancer's breeding ground you are arming. Move away from factory meat, this is not the way to eat. Move away from factory style, meat covered in pus and bile. Move away from factory earnings, undo all your learnings. Move away from factory farming, for yourselves you are harming.

Animals tortured day by day, so that less you can pay. Animals tortured in the mornings, as they go for their de-hornings. Animals tortured in the evening, squashed in pens that are more than heaving. Animals tortured all day long, it's time to recognise that this is wrong.

Closing your eyes to all of the lies, so you can have your burger and fries. Closing your eyes to all of the torture, shutting this down, somebody oughta. Closing your eyes to all of the pain, a practice that is truly insane. Closing your eyes to all of the hurt, whilst animals bleed onto the dirt. Closing your eyes to all of this madness, animals living in pain and sadness.

So much hurt, so much pain, once again for personal gain. So much hurt, so much blood, calves dying in the mud. So much hurt, so much destruction, animals that can no longer function. So much pain, so much waste, back to you this can be traced.

So much greed all around, wasting animals often found. So much greed, so much want, eating more than you can hunt. So much greed, so much gluttony, animals killed not even subtly. So much greed, so much waste, just because you like the taste. So much greed, so little meaning, logic and reason you are not hearing.

Move away from this vile act, it's inhumane and that's a fact. Move away from this vile practice, filling your bodies with prophylactics. Move away from this vile art, polluting the air with the cows' fart. Move away from this vile fact, factory farming should be sacked.

In your hands you hold the power, to no longer make these animals cower. In your hands you hold the choices, you are the masses with the voices. In your hands you hold the reins, to move away from personal gains. In your hands you hold the answers, to move away from manmade cancers. In your hands you hold the knowledge, to do yourselves a great big solid. In your hands you hold it all, to make this practice come to call.

23rd July 2015

Dancing will release your fears, dancing will relinquish tears. Dancing will ignite your soul, dancing will connect your role. Dancing will make your heart feel light, dancing will make you scream with delight. Dancing will make your eyes shine bright, dancing will make your feet feel light. Dancing will much pleasure bring, dancing will change everything.

Reconnect with your inner child, no longer will your heart feel riled. Reconnect with your inner beauty, allow yourself to feel a little fruity. Reconnect with your inner mission, this should be an easy decision. Reconnect with your inner love, reconnect with God above.

Happiness invite back in, at the top of your voice you should sing. Reconnect with your joy, no longer feel shy and coy. Happiness invite to your life, move away from trouble and strife. Reconnect to your inner peace, start to live your life with ease. Happiness invite to your self, put fear and loathing back on the shelf. Reconnect with your inner light, happiness will be in sight.

Such simple things must you do, to feel the joy come back to you. Such simple things must you change, for inner love to not feel strange. Such simple things must you move, for your sadness to be soothed. Such simple things must you bring, to change the crux of everything.

So much fear in your hearts, stopping you from playing your parts. So much anger in your bones, keeping you chained to your homes. So much hatred in your lives, your true selves you keep chastised. So much frustration in your days, keeping you in your demented haze.

Move back into a state of peace, past demons you should release. Move back into a state of joy, make love your favourite toy. Move back into a state of wisdom, soon your lives you will fully live them. Move back into a state of play, remember how it feels to be happy and gay. Move back into a state of freedom, society's chains you no longer need them. Move back into a state of truth, reconnect with your youth.

Soon you will all see, that you have always held the key. Soon you will all know, that sadness you can throw. Soon you will all get, that in your ways you have been set. Soon you will all see, that happiness comes when you simply be. Soon you will all accept, that your soul is never out of depth. Soon you will all discover, that you're connected to one another.

Hurting another hurts yourself, unity consciousness has such stealth. Hurting another hurts mankind, to help yourself, to others be kind. Hurting another hurts the Earth, the wave of anger you all do surf. Hurting another hurts the trees, as humanity crashes to its knees. Hurting another hurts the skies, as love for the planet slowly dies. Hurting another hurts you all, as the vibration starts to fall.

Love will always see you through, love will show what you need to do. Love will always light the way, guiding like the sunshine's ray. Love will always clear the path, to change what's been created with wrath. Love will always win the fight, love will give the gift of sight. Love will always stand so tall, love will make hate break and fall. Love will always lead the charge, together in love you will be large. Love will always conquer fear, love will fill the world with cheer.

Such simple changes must you make, fear and loathing you can break. Such simple changes must you do, to feel the love come back to you. Such simple changes must you be, a better world you will start to see. Such simple changes must you invoke, the fire of unity you will stoke. Such simple changes must you bring, the world together will start to sing. Such simple changes must you start, by simply living from the heart.

24th July 2015

Betrayal runs deep to the soul, betrayal leaves such a hole. Betrayal strips a heart of trust, betrayal often born of lust. Betrayal runs a knife through the heart, betrayal strips a life of art. Betrayal makes a heart bleed, betrayal plants the mind with a seed. Betrayal brings love to its knees, betrayal only destruction sees.

The human race has come to know, love that's often just for show. The human race has come to see, the giving of hearts that are not free. The human race has come to face, a time when love's no longer chaste. The human race has come to be, when love can be bought for a fee. The human race has come to pass, when love is given way too fast. The human race has come to ask, when love is given from behind a mask.

Fast love and fast cars, often hooking up in bars. Fast love and fast drinks, often clouding the way you think. Fast love and fast moves, trying to walk in others' shoes. Fast love and fast proposals, rarely faithful to the ones you've chosen. Fast love and fast disasters, trying to heal your hearts with plasters. Fast love and fast breaks, slow it down for your own sakes.

Never giving yourselves the chance to heal, never allowing the pain to be real. Never giving yourselves a chance to stop, into the next bed you quickly hop. Never giving yourselves a chance to be, hitting on the next one that you see. Never giving yourselves a chance to know, into the next thing you quickly go. Never giving yourselves a chance to sigh, never allowing yourselves a chance to cry.

Others' tears heal your pain, as a blackened heart you start to train. Others' pain soothes your soul, as your darkness takes its toll. Others' hurt feeds your heart, as you're hit by the attraction dart. Others' feelings become unreal, as another heart you do steal. Others' hearts matter not, as your own heart starts to rot. Others' lives fade away, as your wondering eye starts to stray. Others' needs get passed by, as you feed them another lie. Others' dreams slowly fade, as you're thinking about getting laid.

You hurt each other when you stray, so much to lose from a roll in the hay. You hurt each other when you break, the sacred vows that you did take. You hurt each other when you lie, always asking for another try. You hurt each other when you need, to overly spread your seed.

Slow things down, feel your pain, then your heart you will not strain. Slow things down, process your hurt, no longer kick others to the dirt. Slow things down, know yourself, connect to your own spiritual wealth. Slow things down, hear your soul, with self-love fill the hole. Slow things down, be alone, your own love is not on loan. Slow things down, heal your heart, then you'll be ready for a brand new start.

Trust comes from one that's whole, then true love is the goal. Trust comes from one that's not broken, honest words can then be spoken. Trust comes from one that's true, to themselves through and through. Trust comes from one who knows, what their heart truly shows. Trust comes from one that needs, only the path that their soul leads. Trust comes from one who goes, to the place where their soul grows. Trust comes from one who sees, true love won't bring you to your knees.

Broken attracts broken too, it's like the same foot of a shoe. Broken attracts broken more, this is part of the attraction law. Broken attracts broken minds, getting you in all kinds of binds. Broken attracts broken hearts, fix your-selves, use your smarts. Get back to a place that's whole, spend some time with your soul. Get back to a place of self-worth, reconnect with the Earth. Get back to a place of self-love, reconnect with God above. Get back to a place of glory, rewrite your love story. Get back to a place of honour, fake love will soon be a goner. Get back to a place of truth, back to your heart you will move. Get back to a place of peace, no longer feel the love decrease. Get back to a place of knowing, only your true self will be showing. Get back to a place that's freer, then your true self love will mirror.

25th July 2015

Best friends are hard to find, you know, the ones that are truly kind. Best friends are hard to beat, the ones who never allow defeat. Best friends are hard to be, into each other you truly see. Best friends are very rare, to find the ones who truly care.

So wrapped up in personal gain, so much so they have no shame. So wrapped up in their dramas, often being the perfect charmers. So wrapped up in their hurt, your needs they often skirt. So wrapped up in themselves, true intentions are withheld. So wrapped up in their stories, wrapped up in their personal glories. So wrapped up in their moves, not good friends this often proves.

Cherish those who truly are, those who love you near and far. Cherish those who truly give, the ones who care that you live. Cherish those who truly see, the beauty of you and me. Cherish those who truly speak, who give the knowledge that you seek. Cherish those who let you be, the ones that let your heart be free.

So much control comes from friends, often driving you round the bend. So much control given in love, a different direction they try to shove. So much control comes from fear, your dreams they do not hear. So much control comes from thinking, a different path means you're sinking. So much control comes from not knowing, a different tapestry is what you are sewing. So much control comes from seeing, that you have a different way of being. So much control comes from self, in their dreams they are engulfed. So much control comes from passion, from wanting to mould you in their fashion. So much control comes from thought, because you're different to what they were taught.

Learn to embrace your different ways, listen to what each other says. Learn to accept who you are, with the same brush do not tar. Learn to be who you feel, then you'll know what is real. Learn to know what you want, your true self do not shun. Learn to follow your own path, embrace the gifts that you have. Learn to be who you are, then you'll purr like a brand new car.

Help and guidance is just fine, but often friends cross the line. Often thinking they know what's best, not prepared to give it a rest. Often thinking they can guide your way, often having so much to say. Often thinking they need to intervene, not knowing that they're being mean. Often thinking they know a better path, but they don't see the aftermath.

To your soul you must be true, no one can tell you what you need to do. To your soul you must be honest, before you get lost in the forest. To your soul you must be real, only you can truly feel. To your soul you must lend an ear, only you can truly hear. To your soul you must listen, only then will you truly glisten.

27th July 2015

Understand we are all one, know that source we are all from. Understand connected we are, this will help to raise the bar. Understand we walk as one, then differences will be gone. Understand we walk our paths, it's all an illusion, nothing lasts. Understand we discover more, every time we open the door. Understand when we let love in, that will wash away all our sin. Understand when we stand together, illusions of hate will be severed.

Man and spirit walk as one, just ask and it shall be done. Man and spirit blend their minds, spirit is there when man shines. Man and spirit roam the Earth, to many ideas spirit gives birth. Man and spirit sail the sea, spirit helps man know how to be. Man and spirit share their goals, spirit helps to fill in the holes. Man and spirit walk hand in hand, spirit helps man to be grand. Man and spirit walk together, but spirit is always as light as a feather.

The inspiration that you get, spirit has often helped to set. The inspiration that you know, often spirit has helped to show. The inspiration that you have, spirit has helped to hone that craft. The inspiration that you embrace, spirit has helped to your thoughts lace. The inspiration that you bring, into your head spirit sing.

The love of spirit is all around, even though you don't hear a sound. The love of spirit encompasses you, trying to show what you need to do. The love of spirit guides your path, tries to guide you away from wrath. The love of spirit fills your day, open up and hear what they say. The love of spirit fills your world, so many voices not being heard. The love of spirit is always yours, you simply have to open the doors.

Let us in, don't be afraid, once you do fears will fade. Let us in, don't be scared, so much knowledge there is to be shared. Let us in, do not fear, every one of you could be a seer. Let us in, don't turn your back, into our frequency there's no need to hack. Let us in, don't close your minds, open up and see the signs.

You all have the gift of sight, this is your birth right. You all have the gift of knowing, spirit around you often showing. You all have the gift of wisdom, your vibrations you just need to lift them. You all have the gift of power, upon you we do endow. You all have these incredible gifts, but you think they're simply myths.

Stripped away by your churches, the wrong direction everyone searches. Stripped away by your past, these gifts have been downcast. Stripped away by your leaders, of ignorance they are breeders. Stripped away by your teachers, connection to spirit rarely features. Stripped away by your schools, taught a different set of rules. Stripped away by your classes, often nothing more than farces. Stripped away by your rules, disconnection this does fuel.

Re-embrace this special gift, see how it will mend the rift. Re-embrace this ancient knowledge, open up to spiritual college. Re-embrace this ancient right, open your eyes and regain sight. Re-embrace all this power, move away from a world that's sour. Re-embrace this ancient magic, the loss of this knowledge is simply tragic. Re-embrace this ancient way, hear what we have to say. Re-embrace this ancient grace, wiped from your mind without a trace.

Without knowing you all hear, so much to offer if your minds were freer. Without knowing you all see, more to show if you could just be. Without knowing you all share, great wisdom if you would just dare. Without knowing you all get, so much knowledge in your head. Without knowing you all make, intuition is yours to take. Without knowing you all give, a better way for you to live. Without knowing you could all be free, if you would just open your eyes and see.

28th July 2015

Toxic schools, toxic rules, toxic classes, toxic duels. Toxic lessons, toxic nights, toxic sessions and toxic fights. Toxic love, toxic hate, toxic hearts sealing your fate. Toxic lies, toxic cries, toxic drinks and toxic fries. Toxic drugs, toxic thugs, toxic work and toxic jobs. Toxic beats, toxic sounds, toxicity swirling around and around.

So many lies on your lips, deeper and deeper the lie grips. So many lies on your tongue, so many lies ready to be spun. So many lies in your mouths, so many lies you do house. So many lies in your hearts, you don't give yourselves a chance. So many lies buried deep, so many lies you want to weep.

You build yourselves on all these lies, don't even recognise your disguise. You hide away from the truth, worried the world will think you're a goof. You convince yourselves the lies are true, hoping the world cannot see through. You hide away from all the lies, forever chasing synthetic highs. You convince yourselves you're something else, not recognising all your tells. You build your lives on your disguise, self-loathing on the rise.

Deeper into the disguise do you go, working harder to put on a show. Deeper into the lies do you seep, the price you pay for this is steep. Deeper into the spin do you twirl, into darkness yourself you do hurl. Deeper into the act do you fall, never hearing the curtain call. Deeper into the dark of night, your true self out of sight.

You're taught to disconnect at school, playing to someone else's rule. You're taught to disconnect by mates, taking on others' traits. You're taught to disconnect in classes, laughed at cos you're wearing glasses. You're taught to disconnect in the gym, because you sing a different hymn. You're taught to disconnect at play, because you act a little gay. You're taught to disconnect from source, because you take a different course.

Broken people does this make, people acting out in hate. Broken people does this create, trying to take on others' traits. Broken people does this cause, trying to stick to made up laws. Broken people does this push, as their spirit they do crush. Broken people does this see, as their soul's no longer free.

There is a much better way to be, a way that allows you to all be free. There is a much better way to go, a way that allows your true self to show. There is a much better way to walk, a way that allows your truth to talk. There is a much better way to move, a way that yourself you don't have to prove. Simply reconnect with love, reconnect with your Lord above. Simply move back to your heart, allow yourselves a brand new start. Simply reconnect with self, leave your disguises on the shelf. Simply reconnect with source, reconnect with spiritual laws.

Your schools teach you how to be, they tell you exactly how to see. Your schools teach you what to know, into darkness this does throw. Your schools teach you what to believe, from the age that you start to teethe. Your schools teach you how to act, often taking you on a different track. Your schools teach you how to behave, your connection to self they do not save. Your schools teach you how to think, often sending you to the brink. Your schools teach you how to voice, making you believe there's a limited choice. Your schools teach you what to do, heavy hearts coming through. Your schools teach you what to want, sending you on your job hunt. Your schools teach you what to need, often planting the seed of greed.

All gifts should be nurtured, even those that are currently skirted. All gifts should be grown, all talents should be honed. All gifts should be seen as a blessing, arts and crafts and mannequin dressing. All gifts should be treated equal, this is how you nurture free will. All gifts should be treated with love, treated with a kid glove. All gifts should be manufactured, classes should be less highly structured. Science and maths with all the glory, but this isn't everyone's story.

Help those kids with different skills, as their void this will fill. Help those kids with different goals, help them connect to their souls. Help those kids with different dreams, so they're not ripped at the seams. Help those kids with different needs, help to plant their future seeds. Help those kids with different voices, show them a path with different choices.

So much love will this create, no longer acting out in hate. So much happiness will this bring, together the world will start to sing. So much joy will emanate, staying with their own traits. So much passion will this invoke, no longer the brunt of others' jokes. So much change will come about, no longer a need to kick and shout. So much balance will this behold, connecting them to their pot of gold. So much better will this be, to allow a soul to be free.

29th July 2015

Every dog has his day, is something that you like to say. Every dog has his moment, even if it means atonement. Every dog has his chance, his life he hopes to enhance. Every dog has his day, but does it mean he's led astray?

Always searching for power and greed, for these things man has such need. Always searching for power and glory, man is yet to change his story. Always searching for power and more, no matter what you have to endure. Always searching for power and gold, your souls you have sold.

The price for greed is very steep, what you sow you will reap. The price for power is very tall, the higher you climb, the further you fall. The price for hate is very dark, finding yourselves swimming with sharks. The price for violence holds high fees, violent acts will bring you to your knees. The price of pain will run deep, too much pain will make you weep.

Man creates hell on Earth, as he strives for material worth. Man creates hell in his heart, as he adds to his shopping cart. Man creates hell in his mind, as to money he becomes enshrined. Man creates hell in his head, as he strives to make more bread. Man creates hell in his world, as more money he wants to hold. Man creates hell in his arms, as he creates factory farms. Man creates hell in his belly, as many things he sells through the tele. Man creates hell in his path, as a material life he does carve. Man creates hell on his planet, as he drills into the granite. Man creates hell for all, as over money man does brawl.

The Earth's bounty is rich and vast, but many people you have downcast. The Earth's bounty is plentiful and wide, but sharing the resources you haven't tried. The Earth's bounty is strong and tall, plenty of resources to be shared by all. The Earth's bounty is far and long, but used selfishly will soon be gone. The Earth's bounty is deep and broad, but so many resources man does hoard.

So much greed in your heads, storing your money under your beds. So much greed in your hearts, adding more to your shopping carts. So much greed in your banks, never being shared with the ranks. So much greed in your minds, spending it on expensive wines. So much greed in your heads, whilst others walk in bare threads. So much greed in your system, sparkly rings that do glisten. So much greed in your days, never looking for other ways. So much greed in your lives, into darkness this you drives.

The Earth's resources can be pooled, move away from what's unfairly ruled. The Earth's resources can be shared, if only man truly cared. The Earth's resources can be loaned, if only they weren't unfairly owned. The Earth's resources can be used, a fairer way you can choose. The Earth's resources can be loaded, if man's greed was eroded. The Earth's resources can last, if man changes his way fast. The Earth's resources can get back, so people in the world no longer lack. The Earth's resources are there for all, for these resources no longer brawl.

Man always wanting more, making money to the power of four. Man always holding back, worried that giving will create a lack. Man always holding tight, for his last penny he will fight. Man always hoarding stuff, even when others have it tough. Man always striving for greed, even when he doesn't have a need.

Share the love, share the wealth, see how this gets you back to self. Share the power, share the things, see how this makes your heart sing. Share the glory, share your heart, see how this brings a new start. Share the money, share the dreams, see how this happiness brings. Share the resources, share it all, no longer will man need to brawl. Share the food, share the oil, no longer will the Earth spoil. Share the work, share the jobs, no longer will man have a need to rob. Share the land, share the Earth, move away from material worth.

30th July 2015

Open yourselves to different ways, no longer living in a haze. Open yourselves to different reasons, embrace the change of a different season. Open yourselves to different minds, open yourselves to these rhymes.

So much good comes from change, experiencing life in its full range. So much good comes from embracing, the new challenges that you are facing. So much good comes from laughter, the feeling of joy that you are after. So much good comes from seeing, a totally new way of being. So much good comes from knowing, embracing change will leave you glowing. So much good comes from this, soon you'll be left in a state of bliss.

Turn your back on old ways, listen to what your heart says. Turn your back on old hardships, use your love as a harness. Turn your back on old dramas, strip away all of your armours. Turn your back on negativity's plight, open up to the gift of sight. Turn your back on society's trappings, your freedom to be this is zapping. Turn your back on all that you know, then you'll truly be ready to grow.

From the darkness comes the light, then you'll be blessed with the gift of sight. From the darkness comes the gain, then you will all be free from pain. From the darkness comes the love, then life will be less tough. From the darkness comes the beauty, then you'll connect with your karmic duty. From the darkness comes much ease, then life will become a breeze. From the darkness comes the goal, when you reconnect with your soul.

Man always on an eternal search, for ultimate knowledge he has such thirst. Man looking high and low, the search for truth is often slow. Man opening many doors, but often ignoring spiritual laws. Man searching in the cracks, but often missing all the facts.

Looking for answers in the wrong places, always searching in others' faces. Looking for answers in all the wrong ways, buying into the latest craze. Looking for answers in the mist, forced upon you with an iron fist. Looking for answers in manmade places, true words changed in many cases. Looking for answers always the goal, but rarely do you connect to your soul.

Your soul holds the ultimate truth, listen clearly and you'll have your proof. Your soul knows all that's real, it holds everything that you need to heal. Your soul connects you to each other, so many treasures for you to discover. Your soul holds the golden key, connect with it and you will see. Your soul holds all the answers, no longer listen to all the chancers. Your soul will lead you back to self, your soul will lead you to spiritual wealth.

To reconnect with ultimate truth, there are no mountains that you must move. To reconnect with ultimate knowing, you simply need to carry on growing. To reconnect with ultimate wisdom, you simply have to connect and listen. To reconnect with ultimate love, open your arms to God above. To reconnect with the truth of it all, upon your soul you need to call.

31st July 2015

Seeing through open eyes, seeing through all the lies. Seeing with an open mind, leaving your teachings far behind. Seeing with an open heart, reconnecting with your art. Seeing from a whole new view, seeing what is shown to you.

Soon we will be on our way, to open up to a brand new day. Soon we will all walk together, sister, man, boy and brother. Soon we will all stand as one, the dark days will be gone. Soon we will all roam the Earth, as it opens to a complete rebirth. Soon we will walk hand in hand, as we reconnect with the land. Soon we will embrace each other, with the gentle touch of a lover. Soon we will all walk as one, from each other we will not run.

Together we can see this day, open up and have your say. Together we can make this be, with the strength of an old oak tree. Together we can conquer mountains, as we drink from the spiritual fountain. Together we can take this course, never will we need to force. Together we can walk this plane, no longer holding our heads in shame. Together we can walk as one, current division will be gone. Together we can change man's fate, to do this it's not too late.

Man and boy can change the course, put an end to violent wars. Man and boy can stand as one, a better world for your son. Man and boy can reunite, stand together with such might. Man and boy can change the fate, no more acting out in hate. Man and boy can change the plight, stand together, no longer fight. Man and boy can change it all, bring down the division wall.

So much violence has man created, for this we must all be berated. So much darkness does man see, as he fights to be free. So much hatred in man's eyes, spiritual laws he defies. So much anger in man's bones, shouting into his mobile phone. So much treachery in man's hearts, for this cause we all play our parts. So much evil in man's minds, to this darkness man is resigned. So much loathing in man's head, always reacting to what another said. So much greed in man's sight, the time has come to no longer fight.

Man has lived this way for years, always reacting to his fears. Man has lived his life in hate, leading the world to its current state. Man has lived his life with anger, to himself he is a stranger. Man has lived his life this way, but now it's time for a brighter day.

As the Earth moves into a higher vibration, come together as one nation. As the Earth moves into its rebirth, no longer argue over turf. As the Earth moves into a different axis, no longer fight over higher taxes. As the Earth moves into a different space, banish hate without a trace. As the Earth moves into a different day, it's time to try a different way.

Impossible changes these may seem, but come together and share this dream. Unity consciousness holds such stealth, come together in your spiritual wealth. Unity consciousness holds such strength, no longer hold each other at arm's length. Unity consciousness holds such might, come together in delight. Unity consciousness holds such glory, come together to change this story.

1st August 2015

Withstanding the test of time, the truth will always continue to shine. Withstanding the test of endurance, of the truth you have my assurance. Withstanding the test of man, providing the world with many a sham. Withstanding the test of greed, planted is the destructive seed. Withstanding the test of power, the truth will open like a flower. Withstanding the test of control, the truth you will find in your soul.

So many lies have been told, lies that left you out in the cold. So many scriptures' twisted words, a way to control and round the herds. So many memories lost to faith, the lost words of the brave. So many words left unspoken, true meanings often broken. So many lies passed around, true words gagged and bound. So many questions left unanswered, so many people left disheartened. So many people wanting more, wanting to know what went before.

Never was a more honest word spoken, than from a man who's truly broken. Never was a more honest word said, than from a man who lost his head. Never was a more honest word whispered, than from a man burnt and blistered. Never was a more honest word choked, than from a man who was prodded and poked. Never was a more honest word uttered, than from a man who was sliced and gutted. Never was there a more honest sound, than from a man about to be drowned. Never was a more honest word screeched, than from a man about to be lynched. Never was a more honest word forced, than from a man about to be scorched. Never was a more honest word taken, than from a man who was utterly shaken.

This is how you got your proof, this is from where you based your truths. This is how you based your lies, to others' will you all did rise. This is how you got your facts, with the help of violent acts. This is how history told, others' minds you did mould. This is how you came to be, caught in the lie that you can't see. This is how you came to know, upon these lies man did grow. This is how you came to open, to a world that's truly broken.

The truth will always conquer all, soon enough the lies will fall. The truth will always find a way, to wash away what's old and grey. The truth will always stand with might, to bring back the gift of sight. The truth will always stand strong, to point the world from what is wrong. The truth will always find its path, a new way it will carve. The truth will always shine through, now that the world can start anew.

Honest words spoken in love, shared with you from God above. Honest words from brave men, speaking of inner zen. Honest words brought to you, see how the love shines through. Honest words from those awoken, so many words already spoken. Honest words from those who know, guidance from God they try to show. Honest words from those before you, with the truth they tried to adorn you. Honest words from many a man, trying to do all that they can.

Now is the time to embrace what's said, move away from what's in your head. Now is the time to hear the rhymes, move away from what's in your minds. Now is the time to take onboard, the knowledge that has been adorned. Now is the time to let love in, the time to wash away all man's sin. Now is the time to connect with your soul, this is the new way for man to roll. Now is the time to embrace one another, then so much will you discover. Now is the time for man to shine, leaving the dark days far behind. Now is the time for man to move, into a totally different groove. Now is the time for man to shake, into a new dawn he will break. Now is the time for man to behold, moving away from what is old. Now is the time for man to love, to reconnect with God above.

2nd August 2015

Get love back on track, love should be on tap. Get love back to hearts, the first thing in your shopping carts. Get love back to souls, filling in all the holes. Get love back to people, no longer feeling weak and feeble. Get love back to lives, happiness on the rise. Get love back to man, move away from society's sham. Get love back to kids, reconnect them with their gifts. Get love back to nations, fill the world with elation. Get love back to all, hear the sound of love call.

Simply move away from hate, this your soul will elate. Simply close the door on anger, no longer let this emotion brand ya. Simply walk away from doubt, no longer will you scream and shout. Simply turn your back on fears, no longer to be ruled by tears. Simply push away the darkness, using love as your harness.

The time is now to move away, no longer will you need to stray. The time is now to rise up, drink from the spiritual cup. The time is now to embrace yourself fully, no longer allow society to bully. The time is now to stand tall, no longer into darkness fall. The time is now to let it all out, release all your fears and doubt. The time is now to walk your path, the time is now to hone your craft.

Every one of you has a gift, a gift that will help to heal the rift. Every one of you has a talent, that will bring the world to balance. Every one of you has a job, that will stop the angry mob. Every one of you has a need, a need to have your soul freed. Every one of you has a role, simply connect with your soul.

Embrace yourself, embrace your gift, from your soul no longer drift. Embrace yourself, embrace your role, no longer let darkness take its toll. Embrace yourself, embrace your beauty, understand your karmic duty. Embrace yourself, embrace your power, in the mirror do not scour. Embrace yourself, embrace your love, embrace the love of God above.

Our love is always yours, even with all your flaws. Our love will always be, there for all of you to see. Our love is yours to take, your heart we will not break. Our love surrounds you always, feel it even in your hallways. Our love is always there, because for man we deeply care.

Find yourself, find your way, from this task don't shy away. Find yourself, find your truth, your soul will hold all the proof. Find yourself, find your dreams, simply follow your life's themes. Find yourself, follow your heart, this will connect you to your art. Find yourself, find your love, find your way to God above.

4th August 2015

Running around here and there, never stopping to look or stare. Running around everywhere, for yourselves you do not care. Running around near and far, always trying to raise the bar. Running around all the time, trying to make that extra dime. Running around every day, sometimes you need to stop and lay.

To your bodies you do not listen, too busy chasing that which glistens. To your souls you shut the door, as more money you try to store. To your hearts you do not hear, busy running around in fear. To yourselves you do not feel, more time you need to steal. To your dreams you do not see, for this you must learn to simply be.

Filling your bodies with prophylactics, trying to ignore your reflux acid. Filing your bodies with all sorts of pills, trying to pretend that you're not ill. Filling your bodies with chemical warfare, natural healing very rare.

Take some time for yourselves, learn to know when you're not well. Take some time to heal your body, learn to know when you feel shoddy. Take some time to feel your pain, then yourself you can train. Take some time to feel your aches, then you can catch it before it breaks. Take some time to know your limits, catch it before it breaks your spirit. Take some time to hear the call, before your body starts to fall. Take some time to hear it out, before your body has to shout.

Prophylactics are not the answer, this is a sure way to increase cancer. Prophylactics are not the way, take some time to rest and play. Prophylactics are not the reason, these your body will eventually weaken. Prophylactics are not the source, good health they do not force. Prophylactics are not the course, eventually you'll end up feeling worse. Prophylactics are not the way, postponing ill health for another day.

Through this your pain you just disguise, serious illness on the rise. Through this your aches you just cover up, then you go back down the pub. Through this your illness you pretend isn't there, of this practice you must beware. Through this the signs you just ignore, until your health is very poor.

Through this your body you do not listen, your body's telling you for a reason. Through this yourself you make things worse, small things become a curse. Through this you cause much more pain, as good health you do feign.

Your body's telling you for a reason, listen up before you're beaten. Your body's telling you to take a break, hear the call for your own sake. Your body's telling you in good time, listen to it and you'll be fine. Your body's asking for your help, to get it back to good health. Your body's begging for you to hear, don't turn your back on it in fear. Your body's showing you the pain, so from more damage you can refrain.

Fix the problem at the source, let the illness run its course. Allow your body to do its job, of this chance do not rob. Fix the problem where it matters, before your body's left in tatters. Fix the problem in good time, allow yourself to enjoy your prime. Fix the problem without prophylactics, brought to you through lobbying tactics. Fix the problem on your own, this a skill that you can hone.

All you have to do is listen, then you'll know the right decision. All you have to do is hear, then the right course will be clear. All you have to do is open, then you'll know how to fix what's broken. All you have to do is link, then you'll bring yourself back from the brink. All you have to do is know, that your body will you show. All you have to do is connect, then you'll know what route is correct. All you have to do is listen, then your body will go the distance.*

---

*Never change or stop any treatment or medication without first consulting with your doctor as this can be dangerous.

6th August 2015

Roller-coastering through life, always getting in trouble and strife. Roller-coastering through journeys, tightly strapped to your gurneys. Roller-coastering through it all, never hearing your soul's call.

Many lessons does life bring, to show you the joy of everything. Many lessons does life give, to show you how to truly live. Many lessons does life show, to help your soul to fully grow. Many lessons does life invite, to show you how to get it right. Many lessons does life invoke, your spiritual wealth this will stoke. Many lessons does life face, to show you how to fully embrace. Many lessons does life throw, to show you where you want to go.

Good times and bad times come to you, both of these you must see through. Good times and bad times show their face, often putting you through your pace. Good times and bad times rear their head, often in water you do tread. Good times and bad times a part of life, from life's lessons do not skive. Good times and bad times a part of it all, this is how your soul grows tall.

Embrace the lessons that you see, they will teach you how to be. Embrace the lessons that come your way, listen to what they have to say. Embrace the lessons in your life, from them do not hide. Embrace the lessons in the drama, know how to live your karma. Embrace the lessons in your days, see through the smoggy haze. Embrace the lessons on your path, in the face of adversity manage to laugh. Embrace the lessons in the darkness, see the light through the blackness.

Growing tools these lessons be, a way for you to yourself see. Growing tools these lessons are, wear with pride their spiritual scar. Growing tools these lessons make, love of self is yours to take. Growing tools these lessons show, see the light when you are low. Growing tools these lessons give, teaching you how to forgive. Growing tools these lessons engulf, self-awareness the end result. Growing tools these lessons push, if your spirit you do not crush.

The lessons will come either way, hear what they have to say. The lessons will come into your lives, stand and look them square in the eyes. The lessons will come into your days, find your way through the maze. The lessons will come here and there, so much knowledge for you to share. The lessons will come from near and far, you decide the size of the scar.

Embrace these lessons as a gift, soon you will see your spirits lift. Embrace these lessons as an act of love, given to you by God above. Embrace these lessons as your story, a way to re-embrace your glory. Embrace these lessons as a motion, a way to swim in the spiritual ocean. Embrace these lessons as your journey, a way to see that you are worthy. Embrace these lessons on your path, understand the aftermath. Embrace these lessons in your lives, these will make you much more wise. Embrace these lessons with ease and grace, then yourself you can face. Embrace these lessons, see their beauty, understand your karmic duty. Embrace these lessons in all of their glory, understand your soul's story.

So much love will you feel, as you start to know what's real. So much love will you know, as your knowledge starts to grow. So much love will you endow, as you walk away from the row. So much love will you enact, as you learn what you did lack. So much love will you see, as from chains yourself you free. So much love will you take, as past habits you do break. So much love will you honour, as yourself you do conquer. So much love will you give, as you go through this shift. So much love is yours to take, if you just embrace your fate.

Chained are all the masses, fighting against life's masterclasses. Chained are all mankind, to life's lessons often blind. Chained are all of man, to life's lesson's not giving a damn. Chained are all of you, ignoring what you need to do. Chained are the human form, treating lessons with nothing but scorn. Chained are man and boy, depriving himself of so much joy. Chained are woman and girl, not seeing how life's lessons swirl. Chained are the human race, because themselves they will not face.

Look your hardships straight in the eye, to yourselves no longer lie. Look your demons straight in the face, deal with life with ease and grace. Look your lessons straight ahead, see how fear this will shed. Look your drama full on, see how anxieties will be gone. Look at your life with open eyes, cut your problems down to size. Look at life as a journey, cut yourself from your gurney.

7th August 2015

Once upon a fairy-tale, human lives were not for sale. Once upon a simple time, poisoning another was a crime. Once upon a different manner, greed would see you in the slammer. Once upon a different day, another man would not betray. Once upon a different seed, there was no such thing as corporate greed. Once upon a different matter, profit and yield was not a factor.

Doing things for the need, no such thing as corporate greed. Doing things for the matter, illusions of self this would shatter. Doing things to help another, walking with your band of brothers. Doing things to lead the way, to bring the world to a brighter day. Doing things just because, over cracks this would gloss. Doing things for the whole, living your lives from the soul. Doing things to change the fate, rather than charging an hourly rate. Doing things to help mankind, a better world you would find.

Corporate greed has changed your fate, always causing such debate. Corporate greed has changed your path, illusions of working on your behalf. Corporate greed has changed your way, selling your souls for the pay. Corporate greed has changed your manner, over each other you do clamour. Corporate greed has changed the seed, always trying to create a need. Corporate greed has changed the field, only caring about profit and yield. Corporate greed has changed the pitch, only interested in getting rich. Corporate greed has changed it all, corporate greed needs to fall.

You put such trust in companies, using you to pay their fees. You put such trust in their disguise, never seeing through the lies. You put such trust in this system, buying things because they glisten. You put such trust in the way it is, what's yours is mine and what's mine is his. You put such trust in profit and yield, believing that this fate is sealed. You put such trust in all the lies, propaganda on the rise.

People dying for this fate, compassion for others not a trait. People sick for this need, Monsanto selling their toxic seed. People screaming out for help, whilst others sit on so much wealth. People dying every day, long-term ill-ness this does pay. People falling to their knees, as their assets you do freeze. People dead on their feet, as processed food they do eat. People living their lives in gloom, as corporate profits they go boom. People acting out in hate, can't survive on the hourly rate. People dying in the streets, your purpose here this does defeat.

There is no need for so much power, others' rights this does devour. There is no need for so much greed, contempt for others this does breed. There is no need for so much wealth, at the expensive of others' health. There is no need for so much money, whilst another does go hungry. There is no need to hoard it all, so a company can grow tall. There is no need to take so much. money used as a crutch. There is no need for this to happen, all your lives this does blacken.

Open up to another way, come together to have your say. Open up to a whole new world, where your voices are actually heard. Open up to a different time, where you all have the chance to shine. Open up to a different start, where you live from the heart. Open up to a different story, where you all share the glory. Open up to a different view, it's time for you to start anew.

8th August 2015

Dancing in the moonlight, dancing out of sight. Dancing in backstreet classes, dancing your happiness enhances. Dancing in the crowded streets, dancing to so many beats. Dancing in a crowded club, dancing to step and dub. Dancing with all your friends, your soul this does cleanse.

Open up your heart to joy, no longer be shy and coy. Open up your heart to music, see how this your soul is soothing. Open up your heart to its charm, see how this instils calm. Open up your heart to beauty, get out there and have a boogie. Open up your heart to action, reduce your stress by a fraction. Open up your heart to laughter, happiness will you charter. Open up your heart to dance, give yourself a second chance.

So much energy in this creation, a way to let out pent up frustration. So much energy in this act, from the daily grind this does detract. So much energy in this workout, a way to avoid the workplace burnout. So much energy in this tactic, move away from a life that's frantic. So much energy in this motion, a way to let out so much emotion. So much energy in this move, get yourself into the groove. So much energy in this thing, a way to make your soul sing.

All of you can be great dancers, even without mood enhancers. All of you can shake your bootie, just release your inner beauty. All of you can get down and dirty, even be a little flirty. All of you can release this power, break down your inhibited tower. All of you have this magic, move away from a life that's static. All of you can re-connect, see how your life this will affect.

No need to kick and punch, forget about the credit crunch. No need to hold it all in, just let go of everything. No need to feel depressed, pressure building in your chest. No need to fall to your knees, every opportunity should you seize. No need to be stiff, so much joy will this act give. No need to feel shame, release endorphins in your brain. No need to stay awake, in the morning give it a shake. No need to be up all night, dancing can be enjoyed in the light.

Come along and have a shake, as the morning light does break. Come along and let it all out, before you feel the need to shout. Come along and share your beauty, as you move and shake your bootie. Come along and get down, no longer wear that heavy frown. Come along and enjoy the party, walk away with a glow that's hearty. Come along and feel the vibes, cut your tension down to size. Come along and come together, indulge yourself in healthy pleasure. Come along and feel the love, no longer have a day that's tough. Come along and dance your way, into a much happier day.

10th August 2015

Drugs are the devil's tool, drugs can make man a fool. Drugs are the work of darkness, drugs can leave man in starkness. Drugs are a bitter pill, disconnection they do instil. Drugs are a deepened state, often leading to self-hate. Drugs are the work of man, to live his life as a sham.

Always adding to your disguise, forever chasing synthetic highs. Always going deeper in, so much destruction can this bring. Always hiding from yourselves, disconnected from your tells. Always hiding from the truth, disconnecting when you're a youth. Always looking for the next hit, once you're in it's hard to quit. Always looking for the next high, more drugs you're willing to try. Always looking for the next pill, because your void you try to fill.

Drugs can open up your mind, often seeming that they are kind. Drugs can connect to source, open you up to spiritual laws. Drugs can bring you joy, stop you feeling shy and coy. Drugs can open you up, help you drink from the spiritual cup. Drugs can be your friend, but often they drive you round the bend.

So much darkness in your lives, desperation for the highs. So much darkness in your days, living your lives in a haze. So much darkness in your hearts, as your lives seem way too sparse. So much darkness in your minds, as yourselves you try to find. So much darkness in your sleep, as you go way too deep. So much darkness in the morning, when you're coming down and falling. So much darkness through the week, as you try to find your peak. So much darkness in the bathroom, walking away from the classroom. So much darkness in the streets, sleeping under cardboard sheets. So much darkness in your head, carried around like a lump of lead.

You lose yourselves in the highs, trusting in your disguise. You lose yourselves in the lows, as inspiration no longer flows. You lose yourselves in the madness, highs and lows bringing sadness. You lose yourselves in the charade, your true selves start to fade. You lose yourselves in the journey, memories becoming blurry. You lose yourselves in the darkness, using drugs as a harness. You lose yourselves in your own hype, as you just revert to type. You lose yourselves in your own drama, searching for a place that's calmer. You lose yourselves in your ways, searching for the latest craze. You lose yourselves in the pull. because your lives are not full.

Connecting to the altered state, brings about such debate. Connecting to the altered state, can move man away from hate. Connecting to the altered mind, so much magic you can find. Connecting to the altered state, can help man to change his fate. Connecting to the altered mind, can leave your demons far behind. But using drugs as a form of escape, this your soul will soon rape. Using drugs as a way to hide, soon the darkness will reside. Using drugs as a way to be, soon yourself you will not see. Using drugs as a way to act, from yourself you will detract. Using drugs as a way to change, will leave you feeling a little strange. Using drugs as a way to behave, soon the darkness you will crave. Using drugs as a way to live, your true self away you give. Using drugs as a way to find, to yourself you are not being kind. Using drugs as a way to search, will soon leave you in the lurch. Using drugs as a way to guide, will soon negate your sense of pride. Using drugs as a way to go, into misery will this throw. Using drugs as a way to be freer, will only fill your lives with fear. Using drugs as a way to know, only anxiety will this grow. Using drugs as a way of life, will get you into trouble and strife.

Life is not black and white, life is not about wrong and right. Life is not a test of time, doing drugs is not a crime. Life is not a way to be told, experiences will often mould. Life is not a way to enforce, all of your manmade laws. Life is like a wishing well, sometimes sending you to the depths of hell. Life is like an assault course, helping to connect you back to source. Life is like an apple pie, sometimes moist and sometimes dry. Life is like your favourite pet, the more you love it, the more you get. Life is like a rodeo, better when you go with the flow. Life is like an open field, the more you give, the more you yield. Life is like a butterfly, spread your wings and you will fly. Life is like an open door, so much more for you to explore. Life is like a summer's day, moving away from a winter that's grey. Life is like a galloping horse, sometimes it can go off course. Life is like a steeple chase, sometimes yourself you have to face. Life is like a baby's cry, many things you have to try. Life is like a football pitch, often lanes you have to switch. Life is like a lover's call, sometimes you have to fall. Life is like a train ride, from yourself you cannot hide.

Embrace yourself and all of your truth. into the light will you move. Embrace yourself and all of your dreams, this will enhance your self-esteem. Embrace yourself and all that you are, no longer hold yourself afar. Embrace yourself and all you can be, loving yourself fully is always the key. Embrace yourself and all your charms, see how you release your qualms. Embrace yourself and all of your beauty, no longer live your life so mutely. Embrace yourself and all that you know, no longer into darkness go. Embrace yourself, release your disguise, no longer chase synthetic highs. Embrace yourself and accept your flaws, re-connect with spiritual laws. Embrace yourself and know who you are, no longer let your demons scar. Embrace yourself and embrace your soul, no longer will darkness take its toll. Embrace yourself and embrace your life, into love will you dive.

11th August 2015

Time is a precious tool, time can often be your rule. Time is a precious act, something that you often lack. Time is a precious moment, of which man is not a proponent. Time is a precious gift, often leaving people miffed. Time is a precious honour, never know what's round the corner. Time is a precious feast, never know when it will cease. Time is a precious right, giving you the gift of sight. Time is of precious nature, time will always be your teacher. Time is a precious treat, often met with such defeat.

Always rushing here and there, for the moments you do not care. Always rushing to the next thing, never giving yourselves a chance to sing. Always rushing over town, chasing time like a hound. Always rushing to your next act, making sure you're always on track. Always rushing to your goal, lack of time taking its toll. Always rushing to the next place, missing the beauty in your haste. Always rushing near and far, putting your foot down in your car. Always rushing towards the end, your time to others hard to lend. Always rushing to the post, never time to simply coast. Always rushing your way through life, slicing through it with a knife. Always rushing to get things done, to your head you hold a gun. Always rushing to get where you want, for yourself you never hunt. Always rushing through open doors, never stopping to look and pause. Always rushing to be who you are, with yourself you often spar. Always rushing from yourself, moves you away from spiritual wealth.

So much drama in your heads, often giving you the dreads. So much drama in your lives, an act on which the ego thrives. So much drama in your days, can't see through the smoggy haze. So much drama in your minds, peace and harmony hard to find. So much drama on the box, learning to be as sly as a fox. So much drama, crazy thoughts, in your sleep this often haunts. So much drama, crazy minds, you can run but you can't hide. So much drama, crazy dreams, trying to teach you your life's themes. So much drama, crazy beliefs, come to haunt you under the sheets. So much drama, crazy schemes, hunting you down in your dreams. So much drama, crazy lives, cut the drama down to size.

Take time to reconnect, on your life you will reflect. Take time to know yourself, reconnect with spiritual wealth. Take time to stop and pause, as the madness around you thaws. Take time to hear the call, as your outward barriers fall. Take time to know your soul, take time to fill the hole. Take time to open up, drink from the spiritual cup. Take time to be who you are, no longer hold yourself afar. Take time to love life, no longer live on the edge of a knife. Take time to reassess, no longer will you be a mess. Take time to gather close, embrace the lessons that life shows. Take time to love yourself, improve your mental health. Take time to love your friends, see the message that this sends. Take time to treasure moments, understand your components. Take time to love the days, listen to what your heart says. Take time to love each other, so much more will you discover. Take time to hear the cry, spread your wings like a butterfly. Take time to free your mind, leave fear and worry behind. Take time to hug another, give some time to your lover. Take time to feel the wind, forgive those around you that have sinned. Take time to see the sky, hear the bird's lullaby. Take time to feel the sun, from self no longer run. Take time to know your soul, this is your only goal.

12th August 2015

The world is a beautiful place, so much knowledge for you to embrace. The world holds a beautiful power, so much knowledge it can endow. The world is a beautiful notion, swim in the power of its ocean. The world is a beautiful concept, if you can cut through all of the nonsense. The world is a beautiful thing, so much wisdom it can bring.

You limit yourselves with your minds, closing your minds to all that you find. You limit yourselves with your teachings, magical moments becoming fleeting. You limit yourselves with what you know, never giving your soul a chance to grow. You limit yourselves with your knowledge, believing that your foundations are solid. You limit yourselves with all of your dreams, believing the world is what it seems. You limit yourselves in every way, resigned to a life that is sad and grey.

Man has all the tools, to break away from manmade rules. Man has all the means, to see that things aren't what they seem. Man has all the power, to step into the spiritual shower. Man has all the glory, to see through the manmade story. Man has all the strength, he can go to any length. Man has all the wisdom, in his soul he can find the freedom. Man has all the love, just connect to God above.

You limit yourselves to the how's and the why's, to logical thinking you are resigned. You limit yourselves to the here and the now, anything else is too highbrow. You limit yourselves to what can be shown, of each other's thinking you are a clone. You limit yourselves to what you see, never allowing your minds to roam free. You limit yourselves to nothing but matter, conceptual thinking this does shatter. You limit yourselves to all of the magic, limitations that are oh so tragic. You limit yourselves to who you can be, greatness often impossible to see. You limit yourselves to what you can do, never allowing your soul to come through. You limit yourselves to what you can show, never allowing your soul to grow. You limit yourselves to all that there is, so much wonder do you miss.

Open up your minds to wonder, limited thinking steals your thunder. Open up your minds to fate, know your lives can be great. Open up your minds to glory, understand your soul's story. Open up your minds to power, step into the spiritual shower. Open up your minds to love, reconnect with God above. Open up your minds to magic, see how your life this will enhance it. Open up your minds to freedom, the universe can instil such wisdom. Open up your minds to growth, embrace what this journey shows. Open up your minds to knowledge, the universe is your college. Open up your minds to it all, misplaced teachings will soon fall.

13th August 2015

Free your mind, free your soul, get yourself out of your hole. Free your mind, free your body, move away from feeling shoddy. Free your mind, free your dreams, see how inspiration streams. Free your mind, free your anger, negative thoughts you must untangle. Free your mind, free your tears, let go of your toxic fears. Free your mind, free your life, cut through worry with a knife. Free your mind, free yourself, get back to mental health.

So many worries in your mind, thoughts changing with the tide. So many worries in your head, adding to your impending dread. So many worries weighing you down, making you wear an ugly frown. So many worries deep inside, nowhere left for you to hide. So many worries following you, positivity can't get through. So many worries changing your day, don't know what you want to say. So many worries crushing your soul, a busy mind taking its toll.

Take time to meditate, this your mind will sedate. Take time to be calm, reconnect with your charm. Take time to just be, help your mind to be free. Take time to relax, your brain no longer tax. Take time to be in nature, a walk in nature will never grate ya. Take time to unwind, to yourself be more kind. Take time to stay put, this won't see you in a rut. Take time to just be you, to yourself just be true. Take time to know your fears, move down to slower gears. Take time just to sit, this the spot will soon hit. Take time to love yourself, put your plans on the shelf. Take time to rejuvenate, no longer act out in hate. Take time to take it all in, turn your frown into a grin. Take time to readjust, simply being is a must. Take time to slow down, this will help you wear the crown. Take time to just stop, this will get you back on top.

14th August 2015

Enlightenment is a funny word, but still it's a word that's often heard. Enlightenment is a funny notion, sought out like an illustrious potion. Enlightenment is a funny dream, like the cat that got the cream. Enlightenment is a funny need, taking someone else's lead. Enlightenment is a funny dance, never giving yourselves a chance. Enlightenment is a funny goal, simply connect with your soul.

So many teachings telling you, exactly what you need to do. So many teachings claiming that, what they say is the ultimate fact. So many teachings breeding fear, of this they have made a career. So many teachings showing the way, no room for others to have their say. So many teachings breeding contempt, on division they are hell-bent. So many teachings devouring truth, of your faith they want the proof. So many teachings failing you, trust in self they do undo. So many teachings missing the point, teachers of fact themselves they anoint. So many teachings getting it wrong, searching for a place to belong. So many teachings undoing love, in the name of God above. So many teachings creating war, always a way to have much more. So many teachings to follow the light, but often they don't get it right.

There is no right or wrong, simply follow your soul's song. There is no ultimate way, just listen to what your soul says. There is no single path, just follow the path that your soul carves. There is nothing set in stone, forget the things that you've been shown. There is no black and white, your soul has the gift of sight. There is no one size fits all, listen to your soul's call. There are no division lines, a seed planted in your minds. There are no reasons to fear, dispel the tricks that you hear. There is no fiery hell, a notion that you should dispel. There is no judgement day, for mistakes you will not pay. There is no dance with the devil, taking you to another level. There is no fear and hate, only that which man creates.

Love is the ultimate truth, connect to your soul and have the proof. Love is the ultimate way, to bring about a better day. Love is the ultimate story, to connect man back to his former glory. Love is the ultimate notion, to each other feel the devotion. Love is the thing that's real, connect to self and truly feel. Love is the magic wand, to undo all the wrongs. Love is the driving force, through your veins this does course. Love is the strong oak tree, allowing man to be free. Love is the only way, each other do not betray. Love is the only course, reconnect back to source.

15th August 2015

Saturation of the mind, facts and figures you will find. Saturation of your days, jumping onto the latest craze. Saturation of the market, dumbed down minds are the target. Saturation of your lives, consumerism the thing that thrives. Saturation of your schools, being taught to follow the rules. Saturation of your dreams, only chase what society deems. Saturation of your childhood, taught to be the way that you should. Saturation of your choices, brought to you through different voices. Saturation of your truth, given through convoluted proof.

Lack of knowledge is a weakness, throwing you into the pits of bleakness. Lack of knowledge is society's tool, to keep you living under their rule. Lack of knowledge breeds contempt, sending the world into dissent. Lack of knowledge hurts one another, turning on your misread brother. Lack of knowledge is the power, of those sat in their ivory tower. Lack of knowledge allows control, manipulating thoughts is the goal.

Ignorance may be bliss, but soon goodbye to the Earth you will kiss. Ignorance may be easy, but toxic food will make you queasy. Ignorance may be nice, but bury your head and pay the price. Ignorance may cause less drama, but this will affect your future karma. Ignorance may keep you calm, but soon enough it will inflict much harm. Ignorance may be your way, but at your feet the blame will lay. Ignorance may be your excuse, much confusion does this induce. Ignorance may hold your hand, as you all pollute the land. Ignorance may bring you peace, but their power this does increase.

You are the masses with the choices, they fear the day when you use your voices. You are the masses with the power, to bring them down from their ivory tower. You are the masses with the reasons, to want to see many more seasons. You are the masses with the scope, to trip them with their own rope. You are the masses with the answers, to see your way past society's chancers. You are the masses with it all, to make society come to call.

16th August 2015

Regret is a word that's heard, a different path you would have preferred. Regret is a word that's used, a different route you would choose. Regret is a word that's cursed, to change the past you have such thirst. Regret is a word that's chained, to so much misery and pain. Regret is a word that hurts, but around the issue it often skirts.

Regret is a funny emotion, pulling you into a turbulent ocean. Regret is a funny trait, pulling you into a feeling of hate. Regret is a funny reason, locking you in a self-imposed prison. Regret is a funny wonder, working hard to steal your thunder. Regret is a funny task, keeping you wearing your self-imposed mask.

Everything happens for a reason, embrace the lessons and find your freedom. Everything happens on your path, to move you away from a life of wrath. Everything happens on your way, to allow your soul to have its say. Everything happens in your life, to move you away from trouble and strife. Everything happens in your dreams, to move you into illustrious schemes. Everything happens in your days, to help to guide you out of the haze. Everything happens in your tears, to move you away from a life of fear. Everything happens in your arms, to help you see your true charms. Everything happens all the time, until you eventually see the sign.

The universe is here to help, the universe has such stealth. The universe is yours to master, a life of harmony or a life of disaster. The universe is yours to embrace, take it slow or win the race. The universe is at your call, embrace the lessons or continue to fall. The universe is here to teach, the stars are always in your reach. The universe is here to give, wait to die or really live. The universe is here to make, take the bull by the horns and give it a shake. The universe is subtle and strong, to help you know where you belong. The universe is far and wide, recognise that it's your guide. The universe is near and far, here to help you raise the bar. The universe is deep and steep, what you sow you will reap. The universe is here to do, trying to connect to a heart that's true. The universe is here to be, to help you live from a heart that's free. The universe is here to help, reconnect with spiritual wealth.

17th August 2015

We come into the world with a gentle cry, welcomed with a lullaby. We come into the world with a gentle scream, not wanting to leave where we have been. We come into the world with a gentle holler, not knowing if we'll be a scholar. We come into the world with a gentle shout, in ourselves we do not doubt. We come into the world with a gentle moan, as we take in our earthly home. We come into the world with a gentle cry, as we kiss our memory goodbye.

So much knowledge in your soul, guiding you to your ultimate goal. So much knowledge in your dreams, planting all the relevant seeds. So much knowledge buried deep, information that your soul keeps. So much knowledge in your cells, trying to ring alarm bells. So much knowledge in your psyche, connection to self still unlikely. So much knowledge in your veins, reminding you to release the chains. So much knowledge stored inside, your soul is your internal guide.

Your soul knows what you need to do, the external illusion it can see through. Your soul knows where it needs to go, to your mind it tries to show. Your soul knows where it needs to be, trying to set your mind free. Your soul knows what to plot, it knows how to work with what you've got. Your soul knows where to start, how to get you playing your part. Your soul knows how to lend, in the right direction it will send. Your soul knows what to ask, to help you with your chosen task. Your soul knows how to break, when you live a life that's fake. Your soul knows how to show, when you have sunk too low. Your soul knows how to change, to get you back to your full range.

Your destinies are stored inside, from yourselves you cannot hide. Your destinies are fully mapped, but this doesn't mean that your lives are capped. Your destinies are predetermined, but still your life can be a whirlwind. Your destinies are written down, you already know how to wear the crown. Your destinies are shaped and sized, sit back and enjoy the ride. Your destinies are in the bag, but on your journeys you often lag. Your destinies are rest assured, this is part of spiritual laws. Your destinies are on the map, into self you need to tap. Your destinies lie ahead, your soul has already made its bed. Your destinies are yours to embrace, do it with ease and grace. Your destinies will come to you, then you'll know what to do.

Many paths can you take, always room to make a mistake. Many junctions will there be, different paths will you see. Many corridors with many bends, to different courses your life lends. Many winds in the road, always reaping what you sowed. Many turns along the way, always free to have your say. Many winds and many bends, new challenges being sent. Many doors and many cracks, many routes sending you off track. Many breaks and many stops, many fails and many flops. Many yeses and many noes, many highs and many lows. Many waves and many falls, many halts and many stalls. Many laughs and many tears, many times facing fears. Many nights and many days, many times lost in the haze. Many wrongs and many rights, trying to find the gift of sight. Many losses and many wins, many graces and many sins. Many dances and many fights, being shat on from great heights. Many dreams and many plights, many times fighting for your rights. Many ups and many downs, many smiles and many frowns. Many whispers in the dark, many times awoken by the lark. Many touches by a lover's hand, many times with your head in the sand. Many times with the sun on your skin, many times drunk on gin. Many times feeling pain, many times dancing in the rain. Many times feeling love, many times feeling rough. Many times falling down, many times wearing the crown. Many times with love in your heart, many times with a toxic dart. Many times breaking down, many times out of town. Many times breaking up, many times having a strop. Many times releasing pain, all for your spiritual gain. Many times embracing life, even through trouble and strife. Many times playing your part, as your soul directs you back to your heart. Many times finding your way, through a life that's dull and grey. Many times having your fill, as you express your free will. Many times finding your path, many times honing your craft. Many times finding yourself, many times asking for help. Many times getting it wrong, before you connect with your soul's song. Many times getting it right, before you gain the gift of sight. Many times fighting the urge, before you have a massive surge. Many times not trusting yourself, until you connect to your spiritual wealth. Many times before you see, into your soul's destiny. Many times before you know, this is how your soul will grow. Many times before you see, this is how you will be free.

18th August 2015

Hiding from your deepest truth, always searching for the proof. Hiding from your darkest thoughts, clinging on to what you've been taught. Hiding from your darkest day, twisted thoughts on replay. Hiding from your darkest moment, never actually seeking atonement. Hiding from your darkest dreams, not embracing your life's themes. Hiding from your weakest point, rolling up another joint. Hiding from your deepest shame, disconnected from your pain. Hiding from your deepest cry, giving yourself an alibi. Hiding from your deep torment, getting stuck in life's cement. Hiding from your true self, into self you will not delve.

So much torment, so much angst, crushing you like a great big tank. So much torment, so much pain, often driving you insane. So much torment, so much anger, as you make another clanger. So much torment, so much torture, what has anger ever brought ya? So much torment, so much hate, yourselves you do berate. So much torment, so much risk, going out and getting pissed. So much torment, so much doubt, making you kick and shout. So much torment, so much traction, always causing another reaction. So much torment, so much struggle, so many balls for you to juggle. So much torment, so much fight, trying to inflict your will with might. So much torment, so much pain, yourselves you need to retrain.

Look yourselves straight in the eyes, push away your alibis. Look yourselves head on, into the light that you have shone. Look yourselves in the face, all your traits you should embrace. Look at yourselves in the mirror, look into your soul's river. Look at yourselves in the cold light of day, no longer self should you betray. Look at yourselves in an honest way, find the needle in the hay. Look at yourselves with a fine tooth comb, no longer allow your demons to roam. Look at yourselves through honest eyes, let go of your disguise.

Laying blame at another's door, may be what you did before. Laying blame at another's feet, may be how you explain deceit. Laying blame in another's arms, may be how you accept your charms. Laying blame at another's fate, may be how you accept your trait. Laying blame at another's journey, keeps you tied up to your gurney. Laying blame on another soul, stops you from reaching your ultimate goal.

The journey of self isn't easy, you have to dive very deeply. The journey of self isn't quick, there is no switch that you can flick. The journey of self takes many tries, to uncover all the lies. The journey of self is hard to master, the first attempt will be a disaster. The journey of self is hard to know, so many cracks will begin to show. The journey of self is hard to embrace, your own demons are hard to face. The journey of self will take you places, where you'll see all your faces. The journey of self will take you deep, many rewards will you reap. The journey of self will rediscover, how to be a better lover. The journey of self will help you see, just how happy you can be. The journey of self will help you change, help you break out from your cage. The journey of self is yours to take, old habits you can break. The journey of self is your path, to move you away from a life of wrath. The journey of self is yours to know, your true self will this show. The journey of self will cut the chords, from your mind's toxic swords. The journey of self will release your pain, through this journey you have much to gain. The journey of self will bring you back, from your own personal attack. The journey of self will open your eyes, help you recognise your disguise. The journey of self will be your guide, to help you change your life's tide. The journey of self is the way, to get yourselves to a brighter day. The journey of self is your answer, to no longer behave like a chancer. The journey of self will change it all, self-loathing will come to call.

20th August 2015

Awareness is the key tool, to stop you acting like a fool. Awareness is the key player, to stop your life from getting greyer. Awareness is the key trait, to reconnect you with your fate. Awareness is the key card, to move away from the brush that's tarred. Awareness is the key fact, to change your life to a different tact. Awareness is the key move, to get yourself into the groove. Awareness is the key answer, for you your life to fully master.

Always turning your back on self, never connecting to spiritual wealth. Always turning away from fears, anger's ugly head rears. Always pushing emotions down, putting on the face of a clown. Always pretending to be cool, used as a self-preservation tool. Always pretending to be honest, can't see through the prickly forest. Always pretending to be true, can't see the real you. Always pretending to be your best, never putting yourself to the test. Always pretending to be something else, putting your true self on the shelf. Always pretending to be a martyr, it's time to act a little smarter.

Notice all your little flaws, no one's breaking any laws. Notice all your little foibles, see how they get you into trouble. Notice all your little ways, see how the land lays. Notice all your little schemes, see how they create your themes. Notice all your little traits, see how they turn love to hate. Notice all your little moments, no longer be your own proponent. Notice all your little blunders, see how they steal your thunder. Notice all your little hurts, be aware of your self-worth. Notice all your little heartaches, see the darkness that this creates. Notice all your little pains, rewiring all your brains. Notice all your little rifts, start to see them all as gifts. Notice all your little demons, this is how you will find your freedom.

Awareness is the gift of change, for you your life to rearrange. Awareness is the gift of love, no longer should you huff and puff. Awareness is the gift of beauty, to reconnect to your karmic duty. Awareness is the gift of self, to reconnect to spiritual wealth. Awareness is the gift of truth, no longer act like such a goof. Awareness is the gift of magic, to move you away from a life that's tragic. Awareness is the gift of satin, to help you break your negative pattern. Awareness is the gift of gold, to help you release negativity's hold. Awareness is the gift of God, to stop you acting like a sod. Awareness is the gift of myrrh, no more hardships to incur. Awareness is the gift of stealth, to get you back to mental health. Awareness is the gift of glory, to lead the path to a better story. Awareness is the gift of tact, to help you clean up your act. Awareness is the curtain call, to make your disguises finally fall.

21st August 2015

We all have shadow and light, this is how we learn wrong from right. We all have love and fear, this is how we learn to be freer. We all have love and hate, this is how we open the gate. We all have strength and weakness, this is how we move from bleakness. We all have losses and wins, this is how we relinquish sins. We all have good and bad, this is how we learn to be sad. We all have a mix of traits, this is how we find our fates. We all have dark and light, this is how we regain our sight.

You all must understand, in others' fates you have a hand. You all must recognise, you play a part in another's disguise. You all must learn to know, you help decide what others show. You all must start to see, you teach another how to be. You all must start to believe, your actions choose what you receive. You all must start to find, that another becomes resigned. You all must see your ways, have an effect on what others say. You all must see your actions, have an effect on others' reactions. You all must learn to feel, to help others show what's real. You all must learn to embrace, each and every one of your traits. You all must understand, that another's fate is in your hand.

Choose to see the bad in another, they will be a terrible lover. Choose to see dark over light, this is what they will have in their sight. Choose to see a person's hate, this will start to be their fate. Choose to see a person's darkness, soon they'll live their life in starkness. Choose to see a person's anger, into it they will anchor. Choose to see a person's deceit, soon to it they will admit defeat. Choose to see a person's fears, soon they'll be resigned to tears. Choose to see another's pain, soon they will be driven insane.

Choose to see a person's kindness, soon to hate they will show blindness. Choose to see a person's love, no longer will they push and shove. Choose to see a person's spirit, soon they will step up and fill it. Choose to see a person's heart, soon they'll break the poisoned dart. Choose to see a person's dreams, soon they'll shift their life's themes. Choose to see good in another, soon they'll be the perfect lover. Choose to see another's charms, soon they'll no longer do you harm. Choose to see another's light, soon they'll start to do what's right. Choose to see another's beauty, soon they'll connect to their karmic duty. Choose to see another's smile, soon you'll see it all the while.

Choose to see another's soul, no longer will darkness take its toll. Choose to see another's honour, soon disdain will be a goner. Choose to see love over hate, soon you'll help to change their fate.

You all need love in your lives, this is how the soul thrives. You all need trust and respect, to stop you feeling deeply inept. You all need a good friend, to stop you going round the bend. You all need a solid arm, to help connect you to your charms. You all need love and support, this should be what you are taught. You all need a helping hand, to stop you sinking in the sand. You all need a kind word, to into darkness not be lured. You all need the trust of another, to help you be a better lover. You all need to see with love, treat others with a kid glove. You all need to open your eyes, help each other to be wise. You all need to be kind, better people will you find. You all need to plant the seed, this is how you will be freed.

23rd August 2015

Waking up is hard to do, so many barriers to get through. Waking up is hard to embrace, so many lies for you to face. Waking up is hard to see, a different way for you to be. Waking up is hard to conquer, often feeling like a plonker. Waking up is hard to know, a different way for you to grow. Waking up is hard to master, like ripping off a painful plaster. Waking up is hard to touch, kicking away your faithful crutch. Waking up is hard to beat, becoming aware of all the deceit. Waking up is hard to believe, wondering if your eyes deceive. Waking up is hard to learn, seeing the lies at every turn. Waking up is hard to change, once you have the world feels strange.

Disruption in your daily lives, as you see through all the lies. Disruption in your mind's beliefs, as you recognise all the cheats. Disruption in your daily grind, as more madness you do find. Disruption in the way you do things, as more knowledge your awakening brings.

Madness going on in the world, so much madness being swirled. Madness going on in your lives, logic and reason desperately cries. Madness going on in droves, greed and manipulation grows. Madness going on in places, can't see past all the disgraces. Madness going on in towns, toxins planted in the grounds. Madness going on in nations, manipulated TV stations. Madness going on in homes, can't pay back the mortgage loans. Madness going on in health, creating other people's wealth. Madness is in full supply, madness makes you want to cry.

Worry not, the fear will pass, the devastation will not last. Worry not, the day will come, when you no longer want to run. Worry not, the light will shine, and you will know it will all be fine. Worry not, the day will break, and you will no longer scream and shake. Worry not, the time will settle, in your knowledge you will revel. Worry not, the time will move, when your wisdom you can prove. Worry not, the time is soon, the Earth will have a massive boom. Worry not, the time is now, all these changes you must allow. Worry not, things will change, the rebirth has been arranged. Worry not, all will shift, reconnect with your gift. Worry not, the end is nigh, to all the madness kiss goodbye. Worry not, change will come, hear the beat of the drum. Worry not, love will rule, this will be man's only tool. Worry not, hate will leave, no longer will man need to thieve. Worry not, don't feel strange, soon will come the wind of change.

25th August 2015

Words can be a thing of love, kind words spoken not enough. Words can be a thing to treasure, kind words spoken at your leisure. Words can be a thing of kindness, to others' hearts do not show blindness. Words can be a thing to keep, following others like a sheep. Words can be a bitter tool, often making man a fool. Words can be a thing of darkness, taking away another's calmness. Words can be a destructive motion, pulling you into a bitter ocean.

Words can make a man weep, fall to his knees in a heap. Words can make a child cry, inside he may want to die. Words can make a girl scorn, feeling like her heart's been torn. Words can make a woman shout, filling herself with so much doubt. Words can close an open mind, to others' thoughts you are resigned. Words can steal a heart of love, make you want to push and shove. Words can tear a heart to shreds, fill you with impending dread. Words can make a person shy, build their lives on a lie. Words can make a tortured heart, rob them of their given art. Words can bring a darkened sky, rob a life of a lullaby. Words can bring doom and gloom, for happiness there is no room. Words can turn a life to hate, as a person feels innate. Words can change a person's fate, bitterness they can create.

Speak with love and speak with kindness, know your words could be time-less. Speak with love and speak with peace, words of anger to decease. Speak with love and speak with calmness, know your words may not be harmless. Speak with love and speak with joy, spread your love to man and boy. Speak with love and speak with charm, know your words do others harm. Speak with love and speak with brightness, stop yourself from being self-righteous. Speak with love and speak with honour, others' pain could be a goner. Speak with love and with restraint, a blackened heart you will not paint. Speak with love and speak with ease, to others' hearts don't be a tease. Speak with love and speak with truth, another's heart you will soon move. Speak with love and speak with gladness, don't create another's sadness. Speak with love and speak with glory, help to change another's story.

26th August 2015

So many choices for you to make, what is real and what is fake? So many choices for you to behold, in with the new and out with old. So many choices for you to embrace, trying to make them with ease and grace. So many choices for you to enhance, the world is giving you a second chance. So many choices for you to ensure, choices to find the ultimate cure. So many choices for you to give, a better way for all to live. So many choices for you to share, to show each other you truly care. So many choices are yours to see, now is the time to set yourselves free.

Cancer is a serious business, so many people already bore witness. Cancer is a serious disease, so many lives does it seize. Cancer is a serious flaw, curing it has become a chore. Cancer is a serious fate, bringing about much debate. Cancer is a serious act, it's time for you to change your tack.

Many ways for you to cure, many ways that keep you pure. Many ways for you to try, a need to see through the age old lie. Many ways for you to source, many ways to change your course. Many ways to free yourselves, without creating others' wealth. Many ways to change your fate, many ways that are first rate. Many ways to change your fall, ways that keep you standing tall. Many ways to keep your body, in a way that's not too shoddy. Many ways to cure yourself, and get you back to perfect health.

There is no 'one cure fits all', this is the logic that makes you fall. There is no one perfect way, listen to what your soul has to say. There is no one and only need, this is purely born of greed. There is no one and only position, there are many ways to make your decision. There is no one and only right, a broken system you must fight. There is no one and only course, a need to look at the information's source. There is no one and only reason, that survivors see another season. There is no one and only charge, the choices you have are vast and large. There is no one and only point, there's more than what your leaders appoint. There is no one and only decision, freeing yourselves should be your mission. There is no one and only range, it's time to bring about a change.

Trust yourselves, trust your call, it's time for society's chains to fall. Trust yourselves, trust your soul, freedom is the ultimate goal. Trust yourselves, trust your knowing, intuition will start flowing. Trust yourselves, trust your worth, reconnect with the Earth. Trust yourselves, trust your dreams, disconnect from society's schemes. Trust yourselves, trust your wisdom, learn to make your own decision. Trust yourselves, trust your gut, no longer keep the door shut. Trust yourselves, trust your ways, listen to what your soul says. Trust yourselves and free your mind, then the answers you will find.

27th August 2015

Mirrors are the trials of life, mirrors magnify size by five. Mirrors help to see your flaws, mirrors help to open doors. Mirrors are the way to see, a way to help your soul be free. Mirrors help to magnify, help to uncover your own lie. Mirrors help you to downcast, the negative traits behind the mask. Mirrors help to overcome, from yourself no longer run. Mirrors help to guide your way, your true self to not betray. Mirrors are your biggest gift, for out of darkness yourself to lift.

The flaws you see in all your friends, the ones that drive you round the bend, the flaws that make you want to scream, take a look at your life's theme. The flaws you see in family, the ones that you don't want to be, take a look deep inside, there you will find those flaws reside. The flaws you see in all your lovers, even in your band of brothers, take a look at yourself, you'll see these flaws you do engulf. The flaws you see that cause you pain, the ones that give you a combusted brain, these are the flaws that you need to see, in yourself to be free.

Relationships can often test, often seeing you not at your best. Relationships can scar the heart, hit it with a poisoned dart. Relationships can cause you pain, as yourselves you start to train. Relationships can bring much worry, trying to get there in a hurry. Relationships can break you down, see you wearing a tortured frown. Relationships can break your trust, see you acting out in lust. Relationships are the biggest test, to of yourself no longer guess.

Look into your lover's eyes, recognise your own lies. Listen to your mother's voice, recognise you have a choice. Listen to your father's shout, no longer fill yourself with doubt. Look at how you react, when your friend doesn't act with tact. Look at how you behave, when someone treats you like a slave. Look at how you combust, when your lover acts in lust. Look at how you downgrade, when your friend is getting laid. Look at how you act out, when another screams and shouts. Look at how you go red, listening to what another says. Feel how your chest gets tight, when your lover inflicts his might. Notice how you want to scream, when your friend doesn't follow their dream.

Notice how every cell, starts to ring a little bell. Notice how every nerve, shows you what you want to swerve. Notice how every theme, makes you want to kick and scream. Notice how all these traits, connect you to your own hate. Notice how every move, to yourself you have to prove. Notice how every action, causes you such reaction. Notice how all these things, internal conflict do they bring.

Mirrors are your biggest gift, to help you heal your internal rift. Mirrors are your biggest treat, internal conflict you can beat. Mirrors are your biggest tool, to stop you acting like a fool. Mirrors are your biggest answer, to stop you acting like a chancer. Mirrors are your biggest move, internal battles you will soon soothe. Mirrors are the way to see, how you truly want to be. Mirrors are the way to know, the reality of what you show. Mirrors are the way to live, to see exactly what you give. Mirrors are the way to act, to see yourself for a fact. Mirrors are the way to change, a way to see your full range. Mirrors are the way to go, your true self they will show.

13th September 2015

Illusions, illusions of the mind, to convoluted facts you are resigned. Illusions, illusions of the brain, so much tragedy that's simply insane. Illusions, illusions of your thoughts, deeply instilled in your courts. Illusions, illusions of your lives, tragedy and madness is what thrives. Illusions, illusions in your days, your fellow man you betray. Illusions, illusions fed to you, crazy actions you can't see through. Illusions, illusions all the time, making it easy to commit a crime. Illusions, illusions deeply instilled, with so much hatred your head's been filled. Illusions, illusions created by man, love for each other on a ban. Illusions, illusions in your path, treating each other with such wrath. Illusions, illusions in your bones, hatred coming out in drones. Illusions, illusions in your blood, listening to the thrown mud. Illusions, illusions dragging you deep, following others like a sheep. Illusions, illusions, life is cheap, for mankind I do weep.

Invisible borders to be crossed, many a life has been lost. Invisible borders made by man, many borders unfairly ran. Invisible borders causing divide, lucky enough to be on the right side. Invisible borders causing despair, compassion for others very rare. Invisible borders staying locked, respect for life has been lost. Invisible borders corrupting minds, to others' suffering you are all blind. Invisible borders changing fates, buying into others' hate. Invisible borders changing lives, for a better chance they do strive. Invisible borders causing pain, invisible borders are insane.

The world has been unfairly ruled, misunderstanding has been schooled. The world has been unfairly drawn, treating each other with such scorn. The world has been unfairly split, causing so much toxic shit. The world has been unfairly quartered, many a man has been slaughtered. The world has been unfairly divided, with power and greed you have all sided. The world has been unfairly broken, money is the winning token. The world has been unfairly ruled, anger and hatred this has fuelled.

Come together, stand as one, hatred and greed will be gone. Come together, walk your paths, put away your toxic graphs. Come together, love each other, others' light no longer smother. Come together, stand strong, learn to know right from wrong. Come together, open your eyes, listen to a mother's cries.

Come together, don't turn your back, see how much others' lack. Come together, see with love, understand they've got it tough. Come together, share the wealth, reconnect to your true self. Come together, stand as one, unity consciousness shall be done.

15th September 2015

Trying times and trying measures, taking away your earthly pleasures. Trying times and trying means, detracting from your merry dreams. Trying times and trying pains, it always pours and never rains. Trying times and trying themes, seeing you ripped at the seams. Trying times and trying days, walking around in a haze. Trying times and trying jobs, love of life this often robs. Trying times and trying thoughts, so many souls have been bought. Trying times and trying lives, trying to see through the disguise. Trying times and trying gestures, having to listen to so many lectures. Trying times and trying losses, power struggles with your bosses. Trying times and trying nights, getting into so many fights. Trying times and trying points, time to smoke another joint. Trying times and trying rules, taught to you in your schools. Trying times and trying chains, starts to drive you all insane. Trying times and trying moods, toxic drinks and toxic foods. Trying times and trying fates, filling the world with so much hate. Trying times and trying goals, a heavy world taking its toll. Trying times and trying diseases, it's time that the madness ceases.

Reconnect with your gift, see how this will heal the rift. Reconnect with your soul, see how this will fill the hole. Reconnect with your pleasure, see how life you'll start to treasure. Reconnect with your love, no longer will you push and shove. Reconnect with your spirit, open up and really live it. Reconnect with your beauty, understand your karmic duty. Reconnect with all that's true, it's time for you to start anew.

A better life awaits you all, no longer will you want to brawl. A better life is yours to take, move away from a life that's fake. A better life is yours to know, a chance to let your soul grow. A better life is yours to see, of society's chains you will break free. A better life is yours to give, a chance for you to really live. A better life is yours to share, a life where everyone's treated fair. A better life is yours to act, a life where man will never lack. A better life is yours to honour, the darkened state will be a goner. A better life is there for all, just listen to your soul's call.

Live in love and live in joy, no longer feel shy and coy. Live in love and live in honour, all your demons you can conquer. Live in love and live in peace, start to live your life with ease. Live in love and live with dreams, surrender to your life's themes. Live in love and live in freedom, this is how you find the Kingdom.

16th September 2015

Love is a thing to treasure, love finds you at its leisure. Love is a thing to behold, love helps your soul to mould. Love is a thing to keep, but often makes you scowl and weep. Love is a thing to give, love is the only way to live. Love is a thing to embrace, to hold in your heart with respect and grace. Love is a thing to know, a way for you to develop and grow. Love is the key to it all, don't turn your back on love's call.

Love can be a bitter pill, love can make you want to kill. Love can be a ball ache, too many people that take and take. Love can be a heart of steel, not knowing how to truly feel. Love can be a great escape, find your way through the red tape. Love can be a neon sign, love can be a chance to shine. Love can be a heart of gold, love can leave you out in the cold. Love can be many things, so many emotions can it bring.

Learn to open up your hearts, no longer swim in a sea of sharks. Learn to open up your dreams, don't get caught in a web of schemes. Learn to open up your minds, see how the love shines. Learn to open up yourselves, learn to recognise your own tells. Learn to open up to love, slowly does it, no need to shove. Learn to open up to beauty, move away from a life of cruelty.

Love can be a beautiful thing, love can make your heart sing. Love can be a thing of wonder, love doesn't have to steal your thunder. Love can be a summer's ball, love can see you standing tall. Love can be an open heart, love can be a brand new start. Love can be a flower's bloom, love can wash away all the gloom. Love can be a butterfly, love doesn't have to make you cry. Love can be a thing of glory, love can be a beautiful story. Love can wash away the pain, love doesn't have to drive you insane. Love can be like sweet perfume, expand your mind like a magic mushroom. Love can be a thing to treasure, bringing you so much pleasure. Love can be a thing to know, if only your true selves you would show.

Hidden hearts and hidden pain, driving you deeper into shame. Hidden hearts and hidden goals, trying to fill society's roles. Hidden hearts and hidden dreams, making you enact crazy schemes. Hidden hearts and hidden feelings, open up and receive your healing. Hidden hearts and hidden lies, this is how the soul dies. Hidden hearts and hidden notions, getting lost in anger's ocean. Hidden hearts and hidden desires, turning you all into liars. Hidden hearts and hidden traits, turning love into hate. Hidden hearts and hidden ways, walking around in a haze. Hidden hearts and hidden truths, pulling out all your best moves. Hidden hearts and hidden hatred, feelings kept deeply sedated. Hidden hearts and hidden love, making you want to push and shove. Hidden hearts and hidden pain, on your parade this does rain.

It's time to take salvation back, it's time to get love back on track. It's time for truth and love to shine, it's time to leave darkness far behind. It's time for hearts to lead the way, it's time for love to have its say. It's time for peace and love to be, it's time for humanity to be free. It's time for life to shine so bright, it's time to know wrong from right. It's time to speak with open minds, the power of love will soon shine. It's time to speak from the heart, it's time to have a brand new start. It's time to stand together as one, the dark days will soon be gone. It's time to shine the light of love, it's time to know God above. It's time to feel the power of two, love for each other is the glue. It's time to know how it feels to love, into darkness no longer shove. It's time to know how it feels to be, finding love will set you free. It's time to know how it feels to act, to no longer another want to shaft. It's time to know how it feels to give, a better way for you to live. It's time to know what love is, out of another don't take the piss. It's time to know how love feels, as the world gently turns its wheels. It's time to know we are all one, soon the darkness will be gone. It's time to know we can all be, soon the world will be free. It's time to know that things can change, simply feel love's full range.

17th September 2015

So much fighting on the streets, happiness seems out of reach. So much fighting in your homes, anger seeps into your bones. So much fighting in your head, living life in impending dread. So much fighting in your schools, hard to follow society's rules. So much fighting in your lives, resigned to a life where anger thrives. So much fighting in your shows, so much anger in the prose. So much fighting in your towns, travelling in packs like a gang of hounds. So much fighting everywhere, for each other man does not care. So much fighting night and day, another man you will betray. So much fighting in back alleys, always blaming it on scallys. So much fighting in your hearts, all of you play your parts. So much fighting in your blood, always slinging so much mud. So much fighting all the time, life no longer worth a dime. So much fighting here and there, if only the wealth you would share.

Darkness seeps into your bones, taking out another loan. Darkness seeps into your heads, listening to what another said. Darkness seeps into your lives, behind the scenes so many bribes. Darkness seeps into your will, another's wishes you do fill. Darkness seeps deep and far, sinking in society's tar. Darkness seeps far and wide, taking you all for a ride. Darkness is as darkness does, no one seeing through the fuzz. Darkness is as darkness be, the colour of builders tea. Darkness is as darkness knows, a bitter path is what shows. Darkness is as darkness takes, love and happiness it does break. Darkness is as darkness was, hurting each other just because. Darkness is as darkness likes, yet again lightning strikes. Darkness is as darkness sees, can't see the woods for the trees. Darkness is as darkness be, find the light and be free.

Find the light in your soul, no longer let darkness take its toll. Find the light in your dreams, see how following them makes you beam. Find the light in your smile, step into your own style. Find the light in your words, no need to follow all the herds. Find the light in your days, as you start to change your ways. Find the light in your will, so much love will this instil. Find the light in your heart, remember how to play your part. Find the light in all you do, the light will shine through and through. Find the light in all you know, the light within you will start to grow. Find the light in all you see, the light will help you to be free. Find the light and let it shine, darkness will go over time. Find the light and let it soar, man will shine to the power of four. Find the light and let it be, into darkness no longer see. Find the light and let it know, love for each other soon to grow. Find the light and shine so strong, soon the darkness will be gone. Find the light and speak its truth, of its existence you'll need no proof. Shine the light and stand so tall, into darkness no longer fall. Shine the light and shine the love, reconnect to God above.

18th September 2015

Right from wrong and wrong from right, out of mind and out of sight. Right from wrong and wrong from real, forgetting how they really feel. Right from wrong and wrong from hate, with negative thoughts you do create. Right from wrong and wrong from power, building up negativity's tower. Right from wrong and wrong from backward, negative thoughts your minds have soured. Right from wrong and wrong from right, inflicting will with such might. Right from wrong and wrong from real, another's chance you do steal. Right from wrong and wrong from right, wealth is held very tight. Right from wrong and wrong from real, another's fate you do seal. Right from wrong and wrong from right, as for freedom they do fight. Right from wrong and wrong from real, searching for another meal. Right from wrong and wrong from right, no empathy for their plight. Right from wrong and wrong from real, understand how they feel. Right from wrong and wrong from right, purse strings held very tight. Right from wrong and wrong from real, you choose the hand of which to deal. Right from wrong and wrong from right, it's time for you to shine the light.

Hand in hand you should become, stand together, be as one. Hand in hand you should behold, don't listen to what you have been told. Hand in hand you should respect, don't wait until there's nothing left. Hand in hand you can all be, of the chains you can be free. Hand in hand you can all change, move away from a world that's strange. Hand in hand you can remove, others' lives you will soon soothe. Hand in hand you can all form, move away from the hectic storm. Hand in hand you can stand tall, darkness and hatred will soon fall. Hand in hand you can all sing, so much love you can all bring. Hand in hand you can all dance, all your lives you will enhance. Hand in hand you can all love, no need for people to live rough. Hand in hand you can all be, hand in hand you will be free.

22nd September 2015

The power of the conscious mind, can leave the darkness far behind. The power of the conscious soul, can help mankind to find his goal. The power of the conscious dream, can make man work as a team. The power of the conscious thought, can move away from what's been taught. The power of the conscious game, can move you all away from blame. The power of the conscious seed, is the way that you'll be freed.

Man is inherently good, deep down knowing what he should. Man is inherently kind, but to his soul often blind. Man is inherently real, but disconnected from what he feels. Man is inherently nice, trapped inside a game of dice. Man is inherently holy, moving back to self too slowly. Man is a heart of gold, easy to manipulate and mould. Man is a heart of steel, disconnected from what is real. Man is a heart of glory, written is a different story. Man is a heart of passion, but following it is now on ration.

Open up yourselves to love, feel the power of God above. Open up yourselves to honour, hatred will become a goner. Open up yourselves to wisdom, to your soul really listen. Open up yourselves to glory, this is how you change your story. Open up to your dreams, move away from wicked schemes. Open up yourselves to courage, see how inspiration flurries. Open up yourselves to change, no longer feel sick and strange. Open up yourselves to passion, no longer let it be on ration. Open up yourselves to power, step into the spiritual shower. Open up yourselves to peace, start to live your lives with ease. Open up yourselves to life, live in ease and not in strife. Open up yourselves to dance, give yourselves a second chance. Open up yourselves to laughter, learn to be a little dafter. Open up yourselves to fun, seriousness you should shun. Open up yourselves to music, love and laughter you should choose it. Open up yourselves to change, learn to live your life's full range.

The conscious mind is your tool, no longer live like a fool. The conscious mind is your weapon, reality does you beckon. The conscious mind is your goal, this is how you play your role. The conscious mind is your power, open it like a flower. The conscious mind is yours to know, so much power will you grow. The conscious mind is yours to take, move away from a life that's fake. The conscious mind is yours to see, the reality of what you be. The conscious mind is yours to give, a better way for you to live. The conscious mind is yours to hear, connect to it and then be freer. The conscious mind is yours to expand, to understand we're one with the land. The conscious mind is yours to entice, a way to see through all the lies. The conscious mind is yours to enact, to see your minds have been hacked. The conscious mind is yours to embrace, to understand the human race. The conscious mind is yours to open, a way to fix a world that's broken. The conscious mind is yours to know, the conscious mind is yours to grow. The conscious mind is yours to take, do it now for mankind's sake.

23rd September 2015

Pure joy and adulation, is the feeling of the nation. Pure joy and pure love, connected to God above. Pure joy and pure satisfaction, simply spurs you into action. Pure joy and pure dreams, man works together in teams. Pure joy and pure awareness, for money and power you could not care less. Pure joy and pure action, love creates a chain reaction. Pure joy and pure earnest, created is a world that's full of fairness. Pure joy and pure meditation, truth and love on your TV station. Pure joy and pure emotion, hold your passion with devotion. Pure joy and pure laughter, living happily ever after. Pure joy and pure notion, love will be the desired potion. Pure joy and pure work, where disguises no longer lurk. Pure joy and pure knowing, where the soul keeps on growing. Pure joy and pure love, reconnect with God above.

The whole human race needs to understand, that in the madness they play a hand. The whole human race needs to know, the part they play in the lies that grow. The whole human race needs to see, they hold the key to a world that's free. The whole human race needs to react, no longer take lies as a fact. The whole human race needs to feel, into a world that is real. The whole human race needs to seed, mass consumption you do not need. The whole human race needs to love, no longer be tied to society's cuff. The whole human race needs to face, that change is there to embrace. The whole human race needs to act, change is needed and that's a fact. The whole human race needs to be, in a world that is free. The whole human race needs to take, move away from a life that's fake. The whole human race needs to love, reconnect with God above.

So much fear in the face of change, rather live in a world that's strange. So much fear in man's eyes, rather live in a web of lies. So much fear in man's heart, scared to have a brand new start. So much fear in man's minds, to the lies you are resigned. So much fear in man's hands, propaganda through the lands. So much fear and so much worry, corporate greed it does flurry. So much fear and so much woe, material worth is all for show. So much fear and so much anger, into it you do anchor. So much fear and much confusion, adding to the world's delusion. So much fear and so much conflict, into believing you are tricked. So much fear and so much outrage, started is another rampage. So much fear and so many lies, it's time to see through the disguise

24th September 2015

Devastation throughout the land, polluted is each grain of sand. Devastation in your bones, toxins leak into your homes. Devastation everywhere, governments no longer care. Devastation far and wide, nowhere left for you to hide. Devastation in your genes, environment not what it seems. Devastation here and there, more and more big companies dare. Devastation all around, sinking in without a sound. Devastation in your blood, seeping deep into the mud. Devastation and despair, it's time for you to start to care.

The world is made of granite and clay, breaking with each and every day. The world is made of sticks and stones, but every day its heart groans. The world is made of plates of steel, destruction is the thing it feels. The world is made of bricks and mortar, slowly led to its slaughter. The world is made with cast iron power, but its resources man does devour. The world is made with passion and love, but man treats it far too rough. The world is made with a thick iron plate, but show it respect before it's too late.

Toxic poisons in the ground, seeping in without a sound. Toxic poisons in the air, spreading their wings without a care. Toxic poisons in your lungs, toxic flavours on your tongues. Toxic poisons in your bones, brought to you by government drones. Toxic poisons everywhere, fresh air very rare. Toxic poisons in your veins, starting to affect your brains. Toxic poisons in your food, starting to affect your mood. Toxic poisons in your words, following advice of the herds. Toxic poisons in your daughters, take the pill like they taught us. Toxic poisons in your mouths, eating hormone infested cows. Toxic poisons in your days, addicted children do you raise. Toxic poisons in your lives, death and destruction on the rise.

The time for change is nearly here, it's time for you to get into gear. The time for change is on its way, it's time for love to have its say. The time for change is at your door, it's time to hear love's mighty roar. The time for change beckons you, it's time to let the love shine through. The time for change is here and now, before you hear the world go pow. The time for change is in your hands, change is what the world demands. The time for change invites you, to recognise what you need to do. The time for change is at your feet, no longer eat toxic meat. The time for change is yours to choose, there's nothing left for you to lose. The time for change is yours to take, before the world you truly break. The time for change is yours to show, toxins can't be allowed to grow. The time for change is in your hands, no longer pollute your beautiful land.

25th September 2015

Nutrition is the source of life, but into cravings you do dive. Nutrition is the key to health, put the crisps back on the shelf. Nutrition is the key source, to keep you following spiritual laws. Nutrition is the key tool, no longer let cravings rule. Nutrition is the way to go, to stop your body being slow. Nutrition is the key act, to speed up your digestive tract. Nutrition is the key to life, cut through disease with a knife. Nutrition is the key call, to make many an illness fall. Nutrition is the key goal, processed foods take their toll. Nutrition is the way to go, stop your sugars going low. Nutrition is the way to be, from disease to be free.

Processed foods and processed wine, is the way you choose to dine. Processed foods and sugary drink, stops your brain being able to think. Processed foods and fatty oils, no minerals left in your soils. Processed foods and deep fat fried, from these things many have died. Processed foods and ready meals, your energy this does steal. Processed foods and cigarettes, into your cells cancer sets. Processed foods and toxic meat, the purpose of food this does defeat. Processed foods and sugary treats, the digestive system this makes weak. Processed foods and processed minds, never reading all the signs. Processed foods and processed thoughts, changing diet a last resort. Processed foods and processed beliefs, never eating your salad leaves. Processed thoughts and processed ways, sluggish do become your days. Processed foods and processed lives, this is how the body dies.

Take action for yourself, be responsible for your health. Take action in good time, learn to read your body's sign. Take action before you sink, cut out those sugary drinks. Take action, feel your pain, then your body you will retrain. Take action, open up, hear the words of David Jubb. Take action, rehydrate, be aware of what's on your plate. Take action, understand, nutrition and health go hand in hand.

Ease your way into the change, at first it will seem a little strange. Ease your way, set the pace, take time to get used to a different taste. Ease your way into the move, the difference you feel will soon prove. Ease your way, this is a must, soon your body you will trust. Ease your way, know your food, so many toxins have you chewed. Ease your way, change your days, good nutrition really pays. Ease your way, know your body, no longer feel tired and shoddy. Ease your way, embrace the change, no longer feel those tired old pains. Ease your way, trust yourself, get back to perfect health. Ease your way, start today, your good health no longer betray.

27th September 2015 (The blood moon)

Today is a day of wonder, no longer will darkness steal your thunder. Today is a day of rest, will leave you feeling full of zest. Today is a day of change, for man to know his full range. Today is a day to treasure, man will start to know his pleasure. Today is a day to be, the start of a life that's truly free. Today is a day to go, into magic yourself throw. Today is a day of gifts, vibrations will this start to lift. Today is a big day, for the soul to have its say. Today is to be embraced, hate and anger will be chaste. Today is a new start, make sure that you play your part.

The moon and the sun will come to know, inspiration will this show. The moon and the stars will realign, man will have a chance to shine. The moon and the wind will feel the plight, man no longer needs to fight. The moon and the Earth will be as one, hate and anger will soon be gone. The moon and the shore will reignite, man will walk into the light. The moon and the rain will feel the love, man will connect with God above. The moon and the sand will know what's real, man will finally start to feel. The moon and the sun will shine so bright, man will know wrong from right.

Dancing under the beautiful moon, freedom is coming very soon. Dancing under the twinkling stars, Earth will realign with Mars. Dancing in the howling wind, letting go of all your sins. Dancing on a shore of gold, reconnecting with your soul. Dancing through the light of day, love will finally have its say. Dancing together in the sand, dancing together hand in hand.

Man has lived in darkened days, finding his way through the haze. Man has lived in darkened states, the love of God he berates. Man has lived with darkened genes, ripping each other at the seams. Man has lived with darkened hate, it's time for man to change his fate. Man has lived with darkened motives, killing each other with explosives. Man has lived with a darkened soul, now's the time to reach your goal.

Feel the love through the darkness, use the moon as a harness. Feel the love in your soul, dispel the darkness like blackened coal. Feel the love through your dreams, reconnect with spirit teams. Feel the love through your breath, it's time to have a spiritual death. Feel the love through your fears, no longer cry frustrated tears. Feel the love and feel the change, begin to know your full range. Feel the love and feel the glory, it's time for man to change his story.

2nd October 2015

Man has all the tools, to break away from society's rules. Man has all the gifts, to help to heal society's rifts. Man has all the wisdom, to break away from society's system. Man has all the means, to break away from society's themes. Man has all that matters, to fix a world that is in tatters. Man has all the love, to move away from a world that's tough. Man has all the potions, to break away from society's notions. Man has all the ways, to move the world to brighter days.

So much love at your hands, bring love back to your lands. So much love in your hearts, find a way to play your parts. So much love in your dreams, move from what society deems. So much love in your bones, spread the love to war zones. So much love in your bodies, moving back to a state that's Godly. So much love in your arms, reconnect with your charms. So much love in each other, see the soul of your brother. So much love everywhere, for the world it's time to care.

Love is the new vibration, affected is every nation. Love is the new call, see how hate starts to fall. Love is the new way, soon the heart will have its say. Love is the new action, soon to have much more traction. Love is the way to be, soon to be plain to see. Love is the way to go, soon your hearts you will show. Love is the way to live, soon you'll all start to give. Love is the only thing, to make a nation's heart sing. Love is the only tool, to make the world more fairly ruled. Love is what is real, soon the love you'll all feel.

Open up your hearts to love, open up to God above. Open up your hearts to change, no longer will it feel so strange. Open up your hearts to beauty, step into your karmic duty. Open up your hearts to glory, it's time to write a better story. Open up your hearts to wisdom, so much trust can you give them. Open up your hearts in love, open up to God above.

6th October 2015

Peace be love and love be peace, love will make the anger cease. Peace be love and love be more, love will put an end to war. Peace be love and love be real, love will make you really feel. Peace be love and love be laughter, love will bring your ever after. Peace be love and love be all, no longer will you want to brawl. Peace be love and love be true, love will know what to do. Peace be love and love be might, no longer will you want to fight. Peace be love and love be now, love thy neighbour and thy cow. Peace be love and love be always, seeing each other through the haze. Peace be love and love be yours, no longer see each other's flaws. Peace be love and love be you, soon you'll know what you need to do. Peace be love and love be peace, soon the anger will decrease.

Let the power of love come through, soon you'll know what you need to do. Let the power of love soar, through the dimension of another door. Let the power of love ring true, through the door you go through. Let the power of love stand strong, soon you'll know right from wrong. Let the power of love stand tall, hear the power of love's call. Let the power of love guide, anxiety and worry will soon subside. Let the power of love enhance, the world is given a second chance. Let the power of love move, the world slots into a different groove. Let the power of love ring, see the changes that this will bring. Let the power of love be, a different way for man to see. Let the power of love curtail, plots of darkness will soon fail. Let the power of love shine, the world is giving a different sign. Let the power of love be yours, no need to settle old scores. Let the power of love calm, no longer do each other harm. Let the power of love heal, no longer have a need to steal. Let the power of love come through, soon you'll know what you need to do.

9th October 2015

Celebrate a way of life, celebrate getting it right. Celebrate an open heart, celebrate a mastered art. Celebrate love's strong pull, celebrate a life that's full. Celebrate all your gifts, celebrate healing rifts. Celebrate love's young dream, a smile that makes you simply beam. Celebrate an open mind, leaving negativity far behind. Celebrate a summer's day, celebrate the smell of the hay. Celebrate a lover's smile, full of laughter all the while. Celebrate an eagle's soar, hear the sound of the shore. Celebrate nature's smell, listen to an empty shell. Celebrate nature's call, as corporations start to fall. Celebrate a starry night, as the sky is in your sight. Celebrate all your dreams, negativity ripped at the seams. Celebrate an energised soul, as you start to play your role. Celebrate the light of day, as you start to have your say. Celebrate the dark of night, as you start to get it right. Celebrate a thirst for knowledge, living from a heart that's honest. Celebrate a new way, soon there'll be a better day. Celebrate a new start, when man connects to his heart. Celebrate a new dawn, when man no longer lives in scorn. Celebrate a better way, celebrate a better day.

Change is coming in the wind, to wash away all man's sins. Change is coming in the rain, to wash away all man's pain. Change is coming in the stars, to help to heal all man's scars. Change is coming in the sun, to help to change what man has done. Change is coming in the sleet, downward cycles it will beat. Change is coming in the snow, no longer vibrating way too low. Change is coming in your bones, no longer fill your day with groans. Change is coming in the air, move to a system that is fair. Change is coming everywhere, change is coming if you dare. Change is coming in your mind, leave the dark days far behind. Change is coming in your heart, ready to embrace a brand new start. Change is coming in your soul, finally ready to reach your goal. Change is coming, feel the beat, no longer live in deep deceit. Change is coming, hear its roar, man will finally start to soar. Change is coming, know it's here, man will live a life that's freer. Change is coming, know it's real, man will finally start to feel. Change is coming, know it's good, the Earth vibrates as it should. Change is coming, feel the power, step into the spiritual shower. Change is coming, feel the love, reconnect with God above. Change is coming, hear my words, no longer follow sheep like herds. Change is coming, hear the sound, feel the shaking of the ground. Change is coming, know thyself, reconnect with spiritual wealth. Change is coming, hear the call, as corporations start to fall. Change is coming, mark my words, man will be as free as birds. Change is coming, see the plight, into a future that's oh so bright. Change is coming, find your way, know how to have your say. Change is coming, change is now, use the gifts that we endow. Change is coming, change is soon, feel the power of the blood moon. Change is coming, know it is, see the freedom that this gives. Change is coming, change is here, come to know a world that's freer. Change is coming, as it should, change is coming for the good. Change is coming, as it will, many hearts will it fill. Change is coming, hear its call, corporations will soon fall.

10th October 2015

Pride comes before a fall, pride stops you standing tall. Pride plays the hand of fate, pride a man will berate. Pride is the ego's plight, pride makes you think you're right. Pride is an open wound, into ego you have tuned. Pride is a mother's call, as she watches you drop the ball. Pride is the devil's tool, to make you act like a fool. Pride is a father's rule, to keep you well behaved at school. Pride is an act of love, often made way too tough. Pride is an act of lust, never being fair or just. Pride is the work of man, understanding on a ban. Pride is the work of greed, man's ego must be freed.

Deep in ego does man live, never knowing how to forgive. Deep in ego does man bleed, planted is the devil's seed. Deep in ego does man go, his disguise does he show. Deep in ego does man dive, barely even knows he's alive. Deep in ego does man push, logic and reason he does shush. Deep in ego does man weep, it's time to take a giant leap. Deep in ego does man hold, it's time that ego starts to fold. Deep in ego does man jump, making him a massive grump. Deep in ego does man be, it's time for man to be free. Deep in ego does man make, finally ego will start to break.

The Earth vibrates pure and strong, moving away from all that is wrong. The Earth vibrates at a higher rate, it's time for man to change his fate. The Earth vibrates tall and wide, it's time for man to take its side. The Earth vibrates fast and slow, it's time for man to finally grow. The Earth vibrates near and far, it's time for man to raise the bar. The Earth vibrates every day, it's time for man to have his say. The Earth vibrates near the shore, reconnecting with spiritual law. The Earth vibrates, the Earth beholds, leaving behind toxic moulds. The Earth vibrates, the Earth shines bright, it's time for man to know what's right. The Earth vibrates, the Earth is real, soon the Earth will start to heal. The Earth vibrates, the Earth knows, as man's consciousness slowly grows. The Earth vibrates, the Earth sees, as corporate greed falls to its knees. The Earth vibrates, the Earth hears, as man moves away from fears. The Earth vibrates in so many ways, as man finds his way through the haze. The Earth vibrates, the Earth moves, soon to you the Earth will prove. The Earth vibrates every day, it's time for man to have his say.

12th October 2015

Love to live and love to laugh, laughter is the best path. Love to live and love to smile, love and happiness all the while. Love to live and love to share, give your time to those that care. Love to live and love to be, a better way is clear to see. Love to live and love to honour, hatred will soon be a goner. Love to live and love to dance, all your lives this will enhance. Love to live and love to shine, reconnect with the divine. Love to live and love to love, reconnect with God above.

Happiness is in your reach, so many things your soul can teach. Happiness is in your path, move away from a life of wrath. Happiness is in your means, have you feeling full of beans. Happiness is in your power, step into the spiritual shower. Happiness is on your way, listen to what your soul does say. Happiness is yours to take, move away from a life that's fake. Happiness is yours to know, give your soul the chance to grow. Happiness is here for you, your soul knows what you need to do.

Step into your inner self, reconnect with spiritual wealth. Step into your inner knowing, listen to what your soul is showing. Step into your inner wisdom, break away from a corrupted system. Step into your inner mind, leave the dark days far behind. Step into your inner peace, hatred and anger will soon cease. Step into your inner soul, peace and happiness is the goal. Step into your inner light, no longer will you want to fight. Step into your inner spark, no longer act like a shark. Step into your inner wealth, reconnect with yourself.

Self-love is the ultimate goal, here your society leaves a hole. Self-love is the ultimate worth, love thyself and the Earth. Self-love is the ultimate means, moves you away from toxic schemes. Self-love is the ultimate truth, try it and you'll have your proof. Self-love is the one true way, try it a little every day. Self-love is the ultimate prize, consciousness on the rise. Self-love is the way to be, soon yourself you'll be able to free. Self-love is the way to go, soon your true self you will show. Self-love is the ultimate reason, moving into a warmer season. Self-love is the way to go, into love you will grow. Self-love is the way to be, soon yourself you'll be able to free.

13th October 2015

Pictures, pictures all around, silent pictures don't make a sound. Pictures, pictures in your minds, open up and see the signs. Pictures, pictures in your thoughts, intuition you are not taught. Pictures, pictures swirling round, so much wisdom can be found. Pictures, pictures showing you, intuition is the glue. Pictures, pictures in your head, filling you with impending dread. Pictures, pictures all the time, your intuition not worth a dime.

Always stuck in your head, dismissing intuition's thread. Always stuck in your thoughts, intuition never sought. Always stuck in your ways, ignoring what intuition says. Always stuck in your minds, to irrational thoughts you are resigned. Always stuck and always caught, listening to what you've been taught. Always stuck and always blind, a better life you could find.

Intuition is the glue, that shows you what you need to do. Intuition is the reason, to it you all should listen. Intuition is the part, that connects you to your heart. Intuition is the feeling, brings about so much healing. Intuition is your friend, to intuition your time should lend.

Intuition will guide your way, intuition has much to say. Intuition will heal your soul, as it leads you to your goal. Intuition will light your path, stop you doing something daft. Intuition has much to do, keeps your light shining through. Intuition is your gift, from the rubbish you can sift. Intuition is your right, you all have the gift of sight. Intuition in your dreams, showing you your life's themes. Intuition in your heart, helping to unfold your chart. Intuition in your days, helping to unblock the haze. Intuition coming through, showing you what you need to do. Intuition always there, connect to it if you dare. Intuition always yours, as awareness starts to soar. Intuition is your gift, use it to heal the rift.

14th October 2015

People are the thread of life, deep does humanity dive. People are the thread of being, so much hatred we are seeing. People are the open source, humanity driven way off course. People are the planted seed, fallen into destruction and greed. People are the elements, power and greed is what cements. People are the way of life, stabbing each other with a knife. People are the ground force, disconnected from their source. People are the ethereal point, yet church leaders they do anoint. People are the fallen trees, humanity brought to its knees. People are the route of it all, it's time for civilisation to fall.

Hatred seeps into your bones, then your children become your clones. Hatred seeps into your sheets, then your temperament this heats. Hatred seeps into your lives, removing the ability to be wise. Hatred seeps into your eyes, perpetuated by age-old lies. Hatred seeps into your ears, deeper routed become your fears. Hatred is as hatred be, love and laughter you do not see. Hatred is as hatred does, hating another just because. Hatred is as hatred was, inflicting will with such force. Hatred is as hatred comes, looking at another and seeing scum. Hatred is as hatred wants, persecution with your taunts. Hatred is as hatred breathes, continuing to spread this infectious disease. Hatred is as hatred becomes, quickly firing off your guns. Hatred is as hatred knows, your fellow men become your foes. Hatred is as hatred sees, whispered words upon the breeze. Hatred is as hatred shows, as the hatred quickly grows. Hatred is as hatred was, showing another who is boss. Hatred is as hatred be, from this poison man must be free.

See thy neighbour as thy friend, it's time to start a better trend. See thy neighbour as thy teacher, every man is God's creature. See thy neighbour as thy source, no longer inflict thy will with force. See thy neighbour as thy partner, thy enemy thy spiritual gardener. See thy neighbour as thy friend, it's time to start a different trend.

Every man has such beauty, living out his karmic duty. Every man has such grace, many hardships may he face. Every man has such charm, no man should come to harm. Every man holds such light, as the darkness he does fight. Every man has such love, even when he has it tough. Every man holds the key, to find a way to be free. Every man has it all, no need for man to ever brawl. Every man can change his fate, move away from a life of hate.

15th October 2015

Evil hearts and evil minds, to this fact you are resigned. Evil hearts and evil heads, people killed in their beds. Evil hearts and evil ways, so many people feeling crazed. Evil hearts and evil thoughts, high turnover in your courts. Evil hearts and evil breeds, planted are the toxic seeds. Evil hearts and evil acts, trying to cover over the cracks. Evil hearts and evil deeds, into darkness this does feed. Evil hearts and evil means, plotting more toxic schemes. Evil hearts and evil scores, breaking all the spiritual laws. Evil hearts and evil ways, darkness fills your toxic days.

Evil is as evil does, no respect for the fuzz. Evil is as evil be, a better way you cannot see. Evil is as evil comes, to the violence your mind numbs. Evil is as evil shows, soon addicted to the lows. Evil is as evil was, no longer do you give a toss. Evil is as evil starts, so much evil in your hearts. Evil is as evil says, your fellow man you second guess. Evil is as evil tells, plots of darkness is what sells. Evil is as evil be, a better way you do not see.

Find your way into the light, no longer give yourself such a fright. Find your way into the stars, start to heal your toxic scars. Find your way into the sun, past hurts can be undone. Find your way into the Earth, start to know your spiritual worth. Find your way into the sea, soon your soul will be free. Find your way into the moon, start to dance to a different tune. Find your way into the ocean, love will always be the potion. Find your way into the grass, no longer fall on your arse. Find your way into the trees, opportunities should you seize. Find your way into your heart, find your way to a brand new start.

The time is now to be free, open up your eyes and see. The time is now to be found, feel the power from the ground. The time is now to be open, all mankind can fix what's broken. The time is now to be wise, break away from your disguise. The time is now to know thyself, reconnect with spiritual wealth. The time is now to open up, drink from the spiritual cup. The time is now to cut the chains, free yourself from all your pains. The time is now to reconnect, make up with your fellow sect. The time is now to free thy soul, freedom is the ultimate goal. The time is now to love again, no longer feed on other's pain. The time is now, the time is here, to live a life that's much more freer. The time is now, the time is soon, to live your life to a different tune.

The time is now, the time is here, soon enough it will all be clear. The time is now, the time is soon, big changes coming in June.* The time is now, the time is here, no longer live a life in fear. The time is now, the time is soon, powerful was the blood moon.

*Brexit was voted for in June.

16th October 2015

The pitter patter of tiny feet, helps to keep man upbeat. The pitter patter of the rain, slowly drives a man insane. The pitter patter of your heels, as you go to make more deals. The pitter patter of the snow, as the madness starts to grow. The pitter patter of the cars, hiding the magic of the stars. The pitter patter of your breath, as you try to ward off death. The pitter patter of the drums, as the people live in slums. The pitter patter here and there, a life of magic you do not dare.

Magic lives in your bones, too bogged down by the size of your homes. Magic lives in your dreams, too caught up in hectic schemes. Magic lives in your eyes, too drawn in by the lies. Magic lives in the sky, never do you hear its cry. Magic lives in your hands, too deep into sinking sands. Magic lives all around, never do you hear its sound. Magic lives, magic's real, open up and start to feel. Magic lives, magic shines, never do you see the signs. Magic lives, magic's real, open up and start to feel.

Magic is a way of life, into magic should you dive. Magic is a way to love, no need for you to have it tough. Magic is a way to shine, surrounded by so many signs. Magic is a way to be, magic helps man to be free. Magic is a way to go, magic helps a man to grow. Magic is a way to dance, so many lives can it enhance. Magic is a way to open, move from a life that's currently broken. Magic is the touch of a hand, a way to make a life more grand. Magic is the flick of a wand, magic is a day that's dawned. Magic is a baby's cry, magic is a lullaby. Magic is the night's sky, magic is feeling high. Magic is the crash of waves, feeling the beauty of the days. Magic is the power source, man has gone way off course. Magic is the gift of sight, magic leads you back to the light. Magic is the gift of love, connecting you to God above. Magic is the gift of dreams, showing you your life's themes. Magic is the gift of knowing, all the love that we are showing. Magic is the gift of life, which of yourself you do deprive. Magic is the gift of feeling, love exploding to the ceiling. Magic is the gift of being, looking at yourself and truly seeing. Magic is the gift of love, magic is God above.

Reconnect back to source, feel the magic of spiritual laws. Reconnect back to power, your life will blossom like a flower. Reconnect back to glory, change the course of man's story. Reconnect back to wisdom, live a life that really glistens. Reconnect back to nature, live a life that is greater. Reconnect back to love, reconnect to God above.

17th October 2015

Jump, jump, jump to your feet, hear the new world order beat. Jump, jump, jump to your toes, recognise friends from foes. Jump, jump, jump to the moves, consciousness will soon improve. Jump, jump, jump to the tune, changes coming about in June.* Jump, jump, jump to the waves, recognise how they behave. Jump, jump, jump to the party, it's time to think a bit more smartly. Jump, jump, jump to the dance, other's lives they won't enhance. Jump, jump, jump to action, consciousness is getting traction. Jump, jump, jump to the sound, don't be driven by the pound. Jump, jump, jump to the scales, as their plots start to fail. Jump, jump, jump to it all, as the new world order falls.

Slavery has been abolished, that is something that's acknowledged. Slavery has been aborted, a wicked plan that was thwarted. Slavery is no more, as your soldiers go on tour. Slavery is gone for good, just behave as you should. Slavery, a thing of the past, today's life a stark contrast. Slavery is no more, as corporate profits and yields soar. Slavery has left this place, you don't see a single trace. Slavery has gone for good, ask the boys in the hood. Slavery has lost its way, as poor girls are forced to lay. Slavery, a thing of the past, something that could never last. Slavery, lost to history, how it happened is a mystery. Slavery, gone for good, children treated as they should. Slavery is no more, as prostitutes try to score. Slavery, a wicked past, children trafficked very fast. Slavery, a thing that's noted, to burying your heads you are devoted. Slavery, a thing of wonder, so many people's stolen thunder. Slavery has gone for good, sweat shops run as they should. Slavery is no more, manipulated to the power of four. Slavery is gone for good, the world operates as it should. Slavery, a thing of the past, no more people are downcast. Slavery has been abolished, control of others was demolished. Slavery has been aborted, a wicked plan that was thwarted. Slavery is gone for good, you'd believe this if you could.

Controlled are your governed days, towing the line is what pays. Controlled are your governed thoughts, relying on what you've been taught. Controlled are your governed words, following the sheep like herds. Controlled are your TV screens, always following the same themes. Controlled are your written words, papers never as free as birds. Controlled are your very moves, puppeteered like new born fools. Controlled are your daily actions, caught up in mathematical fractions. Controlled are your daily choices, listening to other's voices. Controlled is the food you eat, aimed at keeping you downbeat. Controlled are the drugs you take, keeping you living a life that's fake. Controlled are the jobs you choose, your own soul you start to lose. Controlled are the paths you take, your will designed to break. Controlled are the things you see, so you believe that you are free. Controlled are the things you hear, so you live your life in fear. Controlled are your very days, to keep you lost in the haze. Controlled is your everything, to keep man living in his sin. Controlled is your very mind, to negativity you are resigned. Controlled is your every thought, in the trap you are caught. Controlled is what you do, trapped in society's glue. Controlled is all your life, cutting man down to size. Controlled is the Matrix spawn, the new world order have been born.

*Brexit

19th October 2015

Pretty minds and pretty smiles, wearing the skin of crocodiles. Pretty minds and pretty hair, all the men stop and stare. Pretty minds and pretty clothes, keep the boys on their toes. Pretty minds and pretty bags, scared of turning into hags. Pretty minds and pretty nails, so wrapped up in chasing tail. Pretty minds and pretty moments, affected by your boyfriend's bromance. Pretty minds and petty things, so much tension these things bring.

Testosterone and attitude, no one cares if you're rude. Testosterone and poor judgement, on meaningless sex you are hell-bent. Testosterone and closed minds, in another's bed your girlfriend finds. Testosterone and hangovers, always need to create a buzz. Testosterone and pretty girls, attracted to their pretty curls. Testosterone and big nights out, pushing aside all your doubt. Testosterone and party feet, big nights out end in deceit. Testosterone and party potions, DJs shown such devotion. Testosterone and after parties, loading up on party smarties. Testosterone and deceit, your purpose here this does defeat.

Have fun by all means, fun shouldn't be just for teens. Have fun, still go wild, stay connected to your inner child. Have fun, dance all night, your wild side do not fight. Have fun, be with friends, even buy the latest trends. Have fun, party hard, let down your serious guard. Have fun, be out all night, don't go home until it's light. Have fun, life is magic, don't tap into a life that's tragic. Have fun, let yourself go, this will help the soul to grow. Have fun but keep it real, don't forget how to feel. Have fun but stay on track, don't move into things like crack. Have fun but know yourself, don't forget your spiritual wealth. Have fun but be kind, don't leave respect far behind. Have fun but treat others, know that they're your band of brothers. Have fun but stay focused, don't become a pack of locusts. Have fun but keep in mind, still yourself you must find.

Getting lost in deceit, crashing down at your feet. Getting lost in all your toys, forever chasing naughty boys. Getting lost in sweet perfume, trying to cover the smell of gloom. Getting lost in latest fads, after parties at your pads. Getting lost in your heads, Monday's always filled with dread. Getting lost in your ways, honesty never pays. Getting lost in your glory, often treating others poorly. Getting lost in your haze, jumping onto the latest craze. Getting lost in a club, always drinking down the pub. Getting lost in your lives, cheating on your lovely wives. Getting lost in your dreams, life is never what it seems. Getting lost then getting fucked, into this cycle you are sucked.

Find yourself and find your way, allow your soul to have its say. Find yourself and find your path, a balanced life you can carve. Find yourself and find your purpose, a thing to do with your time that's surplus. Find yourself and find your knowing, allow your soul to keep on growing. Find yourself and find your means, you don't have to do what society deems. Find yourself and find your love, hard to do when you feel rough. Find yourself and find your wisdom, break away from your current system. Find yourself and find your heart, reconnect to your true art. Find yourself and find your courage, then your heart will start to flourish. Find yourself and find your way, no longer have a dull day. Find yourself and find your moment, no longer be such a showman. Find yourself and find your knowing, your true self you will start showing. Find yourself and find your dreams, no longer ripped at the seams. Find yourself and find your worth, the Earth is having a compete rebirth. Find yourself and find your glory, write yourself a better story. Find yourself and find your way, change is coming any day. Find yourself and find your path, this won't make you look daft. Find yourself and find your wisdom, take this chance that you've been given. Find yourself and find your way, walk right into a better day.

20th October 2015

Feel the rain on your lips, as you dance and wiggle your hips. Feel the snow under your feet, as you move to the beat. Feel the sun on your face, as you dance around the place. Feel the wind in your hair, as you move without a care. Feel the sleet in your bones, as you hear the different tones. Feel the love all around, hear the buzz of nature's sound. Hear the love in your laughter, as you get what you've been after. Smell the love in the trees, hear the buzz of the bees. See the love in the stars, wash away all man's scars. Know the love is always there, know that God will always care. Know that love follows you, always there in all you do. Know that love will lead the way, know that love will always pay. Know that love will wrap you tight, even when it's out of sight. Know that love will lead your path, even when you feel others' wrath. Know that love will shine the light, hold onto love with all your might. Know that love will always be, the thing that sets your heart free. Know that love will always sail, love will never see you fail. Know that love will always come, when you feel tired and glum. Know that love will always shine, reconnect to the divine.

So many faces need to smile, true beauty won't beguile. So many faces need to shine, reconnect with the divine. So many faces need to see, love and truth will set you free. So many faces need to know, the true beauty of what they show. So many faces need to get, true love is the task that's set. So many faces need to behold, out with the new and in with the old. So many faces need to show, the path that makes their soul grow. So many faces need to understand, that harmony is working with the land. So many faces need to look, that many a teaching has been mistook. So many faces need to change, from living a life that is now deranged. So many faces need to smile, change is coming all the while.

21st October 2015

Happiness comes in scores, happiness through all the doors. Happiness comes in moments, as man embraces his atonements. Happiness comes in pieces, as hostility soon decreases. Happiness comes in waves, as with love the streets are paved. Happiness comes in sizes, as mankind dispels disguises. Happiness comes in fours, reconnect to spiritual laws. Happiness is yours to take, move away from a life that's fake. Happiness is yours to know, as your soul starts to grow. Happiness is yours to see, as you start to break free. Happiness is here for good, the world vibrates as it should. Happiness is yours to know, man is friend, no longer foe. Happiness is yours to take, society's chains you start to shake. Happiness is here for good, happiness the way it should.

Man vibrates on higher levels, hatred will soon be dishevelled. Man vibrates in different parts, reconnected with his heart. Man vibrates on higher notions, understanding his devotions. Man vibrates in higher states, reconnected with his fates. Man vibrates in different places, knowing all his airs and graces. Man vibrates with the stars, as he starts to heal his scars. Man vibrates with the moon, change will come very soon. Man vibrates with the ocean, love is now the desired potion. Man vibrates with the trees, humanity no longer on its knees. Man vibrates with the sun, no longer will man come undone. Man vibrates with the Earth, man moves into a complete rebirth.

The time is now to open up, time to drink from the spiritual cup. The time is now to embrace change, no longer will it feel so strange. The time is now to chase your dreams, no longer ripped at the seams. The time is now to spread your wings, hear the tune that your soul sings. The time is now to feel your power, blossom into a beautiful flower. The time is now to love yourself, reconnect to spiritual wealth. The time is now, the time is here, open up and be free. The time is now, the time has come, from yourself no longer run. The time is here, the time is now, no longer eat the sacred cow. The time is now, the time has come, spiritual practice no longer shun. The time is here, the time is now, your soul knows exactly how. The time is here, the time has come, from yourself no longer run.

22nd October 2015

Collect the coal, weld the steel, get the world a better deal. Collect the coal, build the bricks, the tar, the mortar and the sticks. Collect the coal, smooth the sand, cover up more land. Collect the coal, flood the seas, smell the toxins on the breeze. Collect the coal, drill the ground, a way to make another pound. Collect the coal, use it up, go for a pint down the pub. Collect the coal, bleed the lakes, do it 'til it all breaks. Collect the coal, pump the sea, take the honey from the bee. Collect the coal, blow the gas, the world will fall on its ass. Collect the coal, cut the trees, agriculture on its knees. Collect the coal, use it up, another mountain will erupt. Collect the coal, sell it on, soon the resources will be gone.

Factory farms and toxic seed, the world's resources this does bleed. Factory farms and paper trails, the law of nature this derails. Factory farms and chemical plants, uncles often born as aunts. Factory farms and chemical waste, back to greed this can be traced. Factory farms and motor homes, can't pay back your home loans. Factory farms and broken homes, too much time on mobile phones. Factory farms and pharma greed, to other illness this does lead. Factory farms and depleted seas, a way to pay your school fees. Factory farms and firearms, your salvation this does harm. Factory farms and closed minds, distorted logic you do find. Factory farms and toxic food, all those toxins that you've chewed. Factory farms and manipulation, coming through your TV station. Factory farms and tired lies, as the Earth slowly dies.

Free yourselves from these things, so much destruction do they bring. Free yourselves from these chains, start to really use your brains. Free yourselves from this madness, move away from destruction and sadness. Free yourselves from this war, all your soldiers still on tour. Free yourselves from this greed, move away from Monsanto's seed. Free yourselves from what's broken, hear these words that are spoken. Free yourselves from your prison, simply make a different decision. Free yourselves and free your minds, release yourselves from your binds. Free yourselves and free your souls, before the ice melts in the poles. Free yourselves and free the Earth, no more fighting over turf. Free yourselves and free your land, man must walk in hand in hand. Free yourselves and free your chains, your current system is insane. Free yourselves and free your worth, the Earth goes through a complete rebirth. Free yourselves and free your hearts, it's time to have a brand new start.

23rd October 2015

Love is a state of being, always goodness you are seeing. Love is a state of action, giving kindness so much traction. Love is an open heart, always open from the start. Love is an eagle's soar, giving strength to the power of four. Love is an open mind, to oneself you must be kind. Love is a football pitch, when you score you get rich. Love is a flower in bloom, singing a much sweeter tune. Love is a butterfly, on its wings you get high. Love is everything, the power of love makes you sing. Love is the greatest high, gentle as a lullaby. Love is the ultimate goal, it's the yearning of the soul. Love is the very thing, that makes your soul want to sing. Love is the ultimate goal, bring love back to your soul.

Love should be as free as a bird, love should never make you scared. Love should be as free as a song, love should never feel that wrong. Love should be as high as a kite, no need to hold on very tight. Love should be like exercise, together scoring many tries. Love should be like a desert's storm, huddled together to keep warm. Love should be a tip of the scale, total balance will not derail. Love should be a baby's cry, honest truth will never lie. Love should be an open door, accepting each and every flaw. Love should be an eagle's flight, allow the other out of sight. Love should be as strong as an ox, no need to be as sly as a fox. Love should be honest words, spread your wings and fly like birds. Love should be an open sail, never worried that you might fail. Love should be outstretched arms, the touch of the other making you calm. Love should be a sailing boat, never should the other gloat. Love should be these simple things, yet so much hardship your love brings.

Expectations of the soul, to always follow another's goal. Expectations of your minds, only room for one to shine. Expectations of your needs, one holds back whilst the other leads. Expectations of your journeys, strapped to your marital gurneys. Expectations of your actions, cutting your light down by fractions. Expectations of your reasons, shelving your dreams for later seasons. Expectations of your means, fitting in with what society deems. Expectations of your lovers, to be best friends with your brothers. Expectations of it all, quickly love will start to fall.

Allow your love to shine so bright, allow your lover out of sight. Allow your love to lead the way, honest love will not betray. Allow your love to carve the path, your lover's dreams do not shaft. Allow your love to shine the light, don't hold on way too tight. Allow your love to make your dreams, trust and freedom is what gleams. Allow your love to give you strength, true love's rope can stretch any length. Allow your love to let you in, following your dreams is not a sin. Allow your love to take you there, in each other's dreams you both can share. Allow your love to find its way, each other's dreams do not betray. Allow your love to give and take, no longer lead a life that's fake. Allow your love to shoot and score, don't set down a lovers' law. Allow your love to be free, so much happiness will you see. Allow your love to be whole, then you'll reach your desired goal. Allow your love to know yourself, an open passage to spiritual wealth. Allow your love to lead the way, love like this will not be grey. Allow your love to shine the light, no longer will you need to fight. Allow your love to be free, so much happiness you will see.

26th October 2015

Open up and let change in, allow the love to wash away sin. Open up and let things go, this is how the soul will grow. Open up and change your fate, move away from a life of hate. Open up and know your dreams, no longer do what society deems. Open up and change your ways, invite love back into your days. Open up, outstretch your hand, live in harmony with the land. Open up and know your worth, feel the power of the Earth. Open up and let love shine, to each other please be kind. Open up and change your fate, see the magic that you create. Open up and change your ways, bring love back into your days.

Love is a powerful tool, not something you learn at school. Love is a powerful notion, different from a life of devotion. Love is a powerful essence, fill yourselves with its presence. Love is an open heart, as juicy as an apple cart. Love is an open mind, never leaving a man behind. Love is a life of dreams, working together with man in teams. Love is an easy feeling, makes man refrain from stealing. Love is the way to go, love will make the soul grow.

Have awareness day by day, slowly move from a life that's grey. Have awareness of your actions, see the enormity of your distractions. Have awareness of your soul, trying to show you your ultimate goal. Have awareness of your behaviour, awareness will soon be your saviour. Have awareness of your themes, learn to recognise your true dreams. Have awareness of each other, know the needs of your brother. Have awareness of your soul, learn to know your ultimate goal.

Distractions are the devil's tool, to keep man living as a fool. Distractions are the devil's potion, of true self you have no notion. Distractions are the devil's work, responsibilities that you shirk. Distractions are the tool of man, to live your life as a sham. Distractions are the devil's warning, to stop the sun from ever dawning. Distractions are the devil's work, in your lives they always lurk.

Take some time to be with self, reconnect with spiritual wealth. Take some time to know your story, recognise your true glory. Take some time to reconnect, your true self do not neglect. Take some time to mull it over, open like a four-leaf clover. Take some time to know your worth, reconnect with the

Earth. Take some time to be still, no longer will man want to kill. Take some time to be true, knowing thyself is overdue. Take some time to understand, inner wisdom is so grand. Take some time to really see, the difference when you simply be. Take some time to figure out, no longer live your life in doubt. Take some time to know yourself, put distractions on the shelf. Take some time to really see, then you'll live a life that's free. Take some time to really know, then your soul will start to grow. Take some time to simply be, from your chains you will be free.

28th October 2015

People look and people stare, they pass by without a care. People scream and people shout, never knowing they cause self-doubt. People laugh and people cry, living their life as a lie. People moan and people bitch, another person up they stitch. People doubt and people lie, in their bedrooms they do cry. People give and people take, resigned to living a life that's fake. People are and people be, never recognising they're not free. People are and people be, a better way they do not see.

Often wallowing in self-doubt, makes a person want to shout. Not often knowing their self-worth, inadequate feelings since their birth. Often feeling not good enough, bottling up all their stuff. Not often knowing who they are, getting drunk in a bar. Often feeling full of shame, caught up in society's game. Not often knowing what makes them tick, instead they behave like a dick. Often giving up on dreams, pulled deep into society's schemes. Not often seeing all their gifts, causes such internal rifts. Often chasing after things, desperate for their diamond rings. Not often trusting who they are, their inner being this does scar. Often seeing someone else, jealousy is what they felt. Not often knowing their own strength, another's path they walk at length. Often feeling deeply hurt, their own demons they do skirt. Not often showing their true face, scared their true self will disgrace. Often hiding from themselves, causing such internal hell. Not often showing they need help, swallowing a giant yelp. Often waking up in pain, looking out and seeing rain. Not often showing how they feel, the way that society's taught them to deal. Not often thinking for themselves, into madness they do delve.

It's time to lead a better life, no longer argue with your wife. It's time to walk a better path, a better life is yours to carve. It's time to see a better way, your true self do not betray. It's time to live authentically, from the chains you can be free. It's time to know the one true you, wear the shoe that's made for you. It's time to open up your pain, facing it will be your gain. It's time to let your demons out, wash away all your self-doubt. It's time to let your true self shine, don't hide behind another line. It's time to take control of self, deep inside you should delve. It's time to step into your power, open up like a beautiful flower. It's time to know your true self, it's time to know spiritual wealth.

30th October 2015

Children are the driving force, so easily led off course. Children are a summer's day, but to their youth you put pay. Children are the building blocks, so gorgeous are their curly locks. Children are the perfect light, easily their dreams take flight. Children are the starting point, easily swayed to smoke a joint. Children are the perfect dream, doing what society deems. Children are the start of it all, so easily can innocence fall.

Manipulated in different ways, welcomed into society's haze. Manipulated for different reasons, navigated by parents' treasons. Manipulated for society's plight, rewarded with sweets when they get it right. Manipulated from right to left, of intuition there's nothing left. Manipulated from their dreams, until their soul no longer gleams. Manipulated for a purpose, welcomed into society's circus. Manipulated out of sight, for their dreams no longer fight. Manipulated to the norm, connection to self will soon be torn. Manipulated to a halt, self-expression is a fault. Manipulated in many ways, tortured become their growing pains.

Always doing as they're told, conformity does not get old. Always learning new ways, listening to what their mother says. Always changing who they are, manipulation from afar. Always learning new ways, to lose themselves in the haze. Always learning how to be, self-expression is not free. Always learning how to show, as their ego starts to grow. Always learning how to act, into ego and cold hard fact. Always learning what they're taught, but memories are very short. Always doing what they're shown, egos becoming overblown. Always being someone else, as their true self they must shelf.

Allow a child to fully express, more is more and less is less. Allow a child to be himself, stay connected with spiritual wealth. Allow a child to know his soul, knowing self fully is the goal. Allow a child to simply be, allow his soul to run free. Allow a child to know his worth, stripped away at his birth. Allow a child to live his dream, choosing his path is actually mean. Allow a child to shine his light, children have the gift of sight. Allow a child to keep on showing, children have the gift of knowing. Allow a child to follow his guide, stay connected with what's inside. Allow a child to show the way, listen to what he has to say. Allow a child to simply be, this is how he will be free.

1st November 2015

Some are old and some are wise, some still live in their disguise. Some are young and some are dumb, deeply under society's thumb. Some are closed and some transparent, differences are apparent. Some care and others don't, some will change and others won't. Some laugh and some cry, some are sure and others shy. Some love and some hate, some will recognise their fate. Some will dance and some will fly, some will live the great big lie. Some will live and some will die, some society will defy. Some will soar and some will fall, some will hear the spiritual call. Some will be and some will know, some will let their soul grow. Some will ache and some will break, some will feel the ground shake. Some will move and some will groove, as the world starts to prove. Some will see and some will say, some will help to change the day. Some will help and some oppose, some will listen to this prose. Some will hear and some abscond, some will feel that they've been conned. Some will feel and some will think, some will think these lyrics stink. Some may ask and others tell, wondering what we're trying to sell. Some may try and some may buy, some may think it's all a lie. Some may give and some may take, some prefer a life that's fake. Some will change and some will not, some their souls will start to rot. Some will grow and some will shrink, some will really start to think. Some will live a life that's true, some would give their last shoe. Some would share their earthly pot, others hoard everything they've got. Some would give their everything, knowing it makes their heart sing. Some would love and some would die, to uncover the great big lie. Some will and some won't, some do and some don't. Some can and some will, some die whilst others kill. Some open and some close, some will buy into the lows. Some start and others finish, as true self they do diminish. Some come and some go, some are friends and some are foe. Some are real and some are fake, some are always on the take. Some are near and some are far, some will start to raise the bar. Some will shine a golden light, as they use their gift of sight. Some will open up the stars, some will drive expensive cars. Some will know the one true way, some will teach and make you pay. Some will know the one true path, some will live a life in wrath. Some will know which way to go, that love will make their soul grow. Some will know to follow their heart, the way to create life's beautiful art. Some will know to trust themselves, into self they will delve. Some will know to honour love, some will know God above. Some will know to live their dreams, some will recognise their life's themes. Some will know who they are, some will come very far. Some will spread their wings and fly, some will live life's lullaby. Some will open up their eyes, some will see through all the lies. Some will change their wicked ways, navigate their way through the maze. Some will open up their hearts, recognise they all play parts. Some will live in harmony, no longer caught up in man's sin. Some will learn to lead the way, so much will they have to say. Some will learn to understand, to live in harmony with the land. Some will learn to simply be, some will learn to truly see. Some will learn to open up, drink from the spiritual cup. Some will learn to live in peace, the need for war will decrease. Some will learn to embrace, learn to love a different race. Some will learn to forgive, know how to live and let live. Some will learn to share their wealth, some take care of their health. Some will learn to shoulder blame, no longer live their lives in shame. Some will learn from these words, no longer follow sheep like herds. Some will learn from this book, maybe have a second look. Some will learn from this page, no longer live their life in rage. Some will learn and some will not, some will think I've lost the plot. Some will learn and some will grow, some this book will others show. Some will learn and some will change, some will know their soul's full range. Some will learn and some will prove, others' hearts they will move. Some will learn and some will see, how to live a life that's free. Some will learn and some will not, but still it must be worth a shot.

Live in love and live in peace, soon the hatred will decrease. Live in love and live in hope, loosen up society's rope. Live in love and live in honour, hatred will soon be a goner. Live in love and live in knowing, allow your soul to keep on growing. Live in love and live together, live as lightly as a feather. Live in love and love in life, cut through hatred with a knife. Live in love and love in peace, all the anger will soon cease. Live in love and love with reason, soon you'll see a different season. Live with love and love for always, walk through the open doorways. Live in love and love yourself, reconnect with spiritual wealth. Live in love and live for now, this book will show you how.

Read it often, many times, more to find in the rhymes. Read it time and time again, until you find you're totally sane. Read it here and read it there, change your ways if you dare. Read it now and read it then, until you find your inner zen. Share it with all your friends, so much wisdom this book lends. Share it with your family, soon enough they will see. Share it with everyone, insecurities will be gone. Share it with your enemies, even if you think they'll tease. Share it now and share it always, wake the world up from its daze. Share it here and share it there, soon enough the world will care. Share it now and share it then, share it to the power of ten. Share the book and share the love, share the wisdom of God above.

CPSIA information can be obtained
at www.ICGtesting.com
Printed in the USA
BVHW031543130819
555787BV00001B/38/P